CONFERENCE OF THE BIRDS

CONFERENCE
of the BIRDS

A Seeker's Journey to
G⊕D

Farid-Ud-Din Attar

Introduction by Andrew Harvey

Translation and Commentary by R. P. Masani

WEISERBOOKS
Boston, MA/York Beach, ME

This edition first published in 2001 by
Red Wheel/Weiser Books
P. O. Box 612
York Beach, ME 03910-0612
www.redwheelweiser.com

Library of Congress Cataloging-in-Publication Data

'Attar, Farid al-Din, d. ca. 1230.
  [Mantiq al-tayr. English]
  Conference of the birds : a seeker's journey to God /
Farid-ud-din Attar; introduction by Andrew Harvey;
translation and commentary by R. P. Masani.
  p.cm.
  ISBN 1-57863-246-3 (pbk. : alk. paper)
  I. Sufi poetry, Persian Translations into English. I. Masani,
Rustom Pestonji, Sir, 1876-1966. II. Harvey, Andrew.
III. Title.
PK6451.F4 M2813 2001
891'.5511--dc21   2001026558

Typeset in 11 point Centaur
Cover and text design by Kathryn Sky-Peck

TCP

08 07 06 05 04 03 02 01
8 7 6 5 4 3 2 1

CONTENTS

PART FOUR

Reception at the Royal Court, 55

INTRODUCTION

by Andrew Harvey

F arid-Ud-Din Attar, the 12th-century Persian poet, is one of the world's most poignant, astringent, and exalted mystics. His masterpiece the *Manteq-ut-tair* (*Conference of the Birds*) ranks with only a handful of works—the Bhagavad Gita, the *Divine Comedy*, Rumi's spiritual epic the *Mathnawi*—that transcend the temporal cultural conditions under which they were created in order to speak with the unmistakable authority of authentic inner experience to all seekers on all paths. Eva de Vitray Meyerovitch, the great French Sufi scholar and Rumi translator, used to say of the *Manteq-ut-tair*, "All true seekers should read it from beginning to end every three years to see how far they have progressed; it is a divine mirror that reflects back to you transformed what you have come to understand." I have been reading and re-reading *Conference of the Birds* for over twenty-five years now, at every stage of my own inner evolution. With each reading, I have found in it a deeper and more mysterious beauty, and fresh wonders of insight.

Attar was born at Neishapur (also the birthplace of Omar Khayyam) in northeast Iran in around 1120. His name derives from a form of the word "attar"—as in "attar of roses"—which suggests that he was a perfume seller, or a druggist, or perhaps someone who combined the selling of drugs and perfume with the practice of medicine. He was almost certainly educated at the theological college attached to the shrine of Imam Reza of Mashad (a major spiritual center of pilgrimage), and he spent many years wandering the world in search of wisdom. He is said to have visited Rey (the ancient Reghges), Egypt, Damascus, Mecca, Turkestan, and India. After his years of wandering, he settled in his birthplace where he wrote *The Book of Secrets, The Memorial of the Saints, The Hidden Voice,* and other major works, as well as *Conference of the Birds,* which he finished in 1177. No one knows for sure which Sufi lineage, if any, Attar belonged to. Some authorities name his "sheikh" as Majd-al-Din of Baghdad (who died in 1219); others, following a tradition we see first in Rumi, suggest that he was instructed directly in a dream by Al-Hallaj himself, the great mystic revolutionary who was executed for heresy in Baghdad in 922. As any reading of *Conference of the Birds* will reveal, Attar's own mystic philosophy was fierce and scornful of all rational or dogmatic authority; it comes as no surprise, then, that he offended the religious authorities of his day, was tried for heresy himself, and had his property looted, probably in the late 12th century. What happened to him then is unclear. All we know is that he died, old, back in Neishapur, in or around 1220.

Whatever Attar's actual Sufi "status," there can be no doubt about his importance to the unfolding of Sufi mysticism; he is the pivotal figure in Sufi poetry between Sanal in the 12th century and Rumi in the 13th. Aflaur, Rumi's hagiographer, maintains that Rumi met Attar in Neishapur as a child. It is possible. Rumi and his family fled from the Mongols, and left their home in Balkh in Afghansiava in 1217. Aflaur claims Attar was so amazed by the brilliance, purity, and precocity of the young Rumi that he prophesied, "This boy will open a gate in the wall of love and throw a fire on the hearts of all mystic lovers." For his part, whether he met him in person or not, Rumi admired Attar and his work—especially, it seems, *Conference of the Birds*—profoundly and extravagantly. In his *Diwan* Rumi wrote,

> I am the Master of Rumi whose words are perfumed with sweetness. But in everything I say I am only the servant of Attar.

Rumi's son, Sultan Valad, maintained in *The Secret Word* that "Sanal was Rumi's eyes and Attar his soul."

It is not hard to see what permanently moved and enchanted Rumi in *Conference of the Birds*. It is a brilliantly executed allegory of the mystical journey, a work in which, as in Rumi's own odes and *Mathnawi*, supreme literary excellence and spiritual depth of instruction intermingle and serve each other, effortlessly and seamlessly, and with great originality.

The allegorical framework of *Conference of the Birds* has the stark, luminous simplicity of Islamic calligraphy. The birds of the world gather together to look for a king and are instructed by one of the birds, a hoopoe, that the Simurg lives far away and that the journey to him is fraught with dangers. At first, the birds are thrilled, but as they begin to understand how harsh and demanding the journey to the Simurg will inevitably be, they start to make excuses. One by one, the birds—and the different types of human being each represents—start to proffer their excuses. The nightingale claims he cannot tear himself away from his obsession, the rose. The peacock argues that he is quite unworthy of the royal presence because of the part he had played in the expulsion of Adam from Paradise. The duck cannot do without water, nor the partridge without mountains. The heron wishes to stay in the lagoons and the owl in the ruins over which he is the undisturbed monarch.

The hoopoe refutes each of the bird's excuses with stories that demonstrate their fatuity and the hollowness of the fears or desires they express. Inspired by the hoopoe's wisdom, the group begins its journey, adopts the hoopoe as its leader, and then halts again to ask the hoopoe questions about the rest of the journey before going any farther. The hoopoe replies with a string of anecdotes. The birds' final question concerns the actual length of the journey. In profound, gorgeous imagery, the hoopoe tells them of the "seven valleys of the Way": the Quest, Love, Knowledge, Independence and Detachment, Unity, Bewilderment and Stupefaction, Poverty and Annihilation. Attar then passes swiftly over the journey itself to show the last thirty surviving birds arriving at the court of the Simurg.

At first, their plea to see the Great Bird is rebuffed, then they are admitted and the Simurg reveals to them the supreme secret of the Quest—that what they are really looking for—the truth about Him—is also, and miraculously, the truth about their own identity. As he says, "The Sun of my Majesty is a mirror. Whoever beholds himself in the mirror sees there his soul and body, sees himself entire in it. Soul and body see soul and body. Since you thirty birds have come here, you find thirty birds in the mirror." This wonderful climax draws some of its power in the original from a pun; only thirty (si) birds (murg) reach journey's end and what they meet is the "Si-Murg." Attar writes, "Thereupon the birds lost themselves in the Simurg. The shade then vanished in the sun. Finding the Simurg they found themselves and the riddle of 'I' and 'thou' was solved."

In elaborating this brilliant and profound bird allegory, Attar drew on several literary and mystical precedents. The Koran celebrates the spiritual life in all animals and even in inanimate objects. It proclaims, "There is not a single thing that but glorifies Him with its praise but you do not understand that glorification." One of Sanat's odes describes the different cries of birds as different ways of calling on the Divine. In a famous contemporary animal fable—Rudaki's *Kalil and Dimna*—animals talk and act as humans. In Avicenna's spiritual treatise *The Bird*, a bird that clearly represents the soul speaks of being freed from its cage and crossing eight mountain peaks to see its "king." What separates Attar's work from all its influences is the depth of its psychological understanding, the sophistication of its literary devices, its terse, dazzling imagery and its great mystical intensity, complexity, and depth.

From the outset of *Conference of the Birds*, we realize that we are in the hands of a caustic master psychologist of human nature, someone who knows from within all the nuances of the ways we try to evade the rigor and cost of the Path to God. This psychological acuity doesn't simply illuminate the comedy of the objections of the various birds and of the hoopoe's reply; it colors and irradiates the entire work, every anecdote, every intimate mystical description, every twist and turn of the allegory's elaboration. The entire work is lit up by the glittering ruthlessness of a great mystic's self-knowledge—free of all illusion—as if by a great fierce light that leaves no corner of false bravado or vanity unexposed.

This ruthless psychological intelligence is magically reflected in the range and sophistication of the literary devices that make up the poem and keep its pace electric. *Conference of the Birds* is a dance of dazzling anecdotes, some short and savage, some baroque and paradoxical (like the "Story of Shaykh San'an"), all of which open themselves to ambiguous, even conflicting, interpretations. The effect of this dancing sophistication of address is to keep us constantly alert to Attar's shifts of meaning and intentions and to draw us creatively into the heart of the allegory in such a way that we, too, like the birds, are instructed by the hoopoe, his stories, and the turns of the allegory itself. Eva de Vitray Meyerovitch used to say, "You begin by reading *Conference of the Birds* with a certain amused detachment; soon you realize that it is you who are being read."

This strange excitement of "being read" by the poem as it unfolds is greatly enhanced by the "voice" of the hoopoe himself, who is clearly a stand-in for Attar. The hoopoe is fierce, tough, exalted, scathing, exhortatory; he constantly uses pithy, vibrant imagery that makes abstractions and mysteries palpable. Some of Attar's greatest writing—and the hoopoe's most effective instruction—is found in the description of the "valley of detachment" and the uncanny "serenity" it engenders in the seeker:

> Although you see here a whole world on fire, ablaze in its very core, I know that it is no more than a dream. Should myriads of souls be drowned ceaselessly in the boundless deep, it would be like a tiny dew-drop falling into the sea . . . should heaven and

earth be split up into minute atoms, take it that a leaf has fallen from a tree. If everything from the fish to the moon were plunged into annihilation, take it that the leg of an ant has been maimed in the bottom of a well.

The juxtaposition in this passage of vast cosmic imagery with the most exactly observed images of minuteness shocks the reader into starting to understand something of the enormous—and disturbing—grandeur of the total absorption-in-God that Attar is trying to make vivid to us. Only someone who had, in the deepest sense, lived the mysteries he is hoping to convey could describe them with such sensuous intensity. *Conference of the Birds* is encrusted with phrases that burn with a hard diamond-like brilliance:

> Once divine love penetrates the heart of a man, it makes him as brave as a lion, even though he may be as feeble as an ant. How can one who takes a leap into the ocean of adventure accept any drink but the blood of his heart?

The psychological intelligence and linguistic mastery of *Conference of the Birds* would be marvelous by themselves; they are even more startling and moving because they completely serve the mystical vision of Attar, a vision whose ferocity and majesty imbue the poem as it unfolds with increasing splendor. You may believe you are reading a witty, dazzling allegory for a few pages of the *Manteq-ut-tair*; very soon, however, if you are reading with any attention, you will realize that you are being drawn into a vision of the mystical path of the greatest possible depth.

Conference of the Birds isn't simply a poem about Sufism, the esoteric doctrine of Islam that celebrates the unity of God and His creation, the soul and its origin, "lover" and "beloved." It is, in fact, saturated with the sense of paradox and the fiery intensity of the Sufi Path itself. The flaming heart-core of this Path can be found in the following *hadith* or "sacred saying" of Mohammed, from whose "secret teachings" some of the main revelations of Sufism developed. Mohammed is "speaking" in the voice of Allah: "Whoever seeks Me finds Me and whoever finds Me comes to know Me and whoever comes to know Me loves Me and whoever loves Me then I kill that person and whomsoever I kill then I must pay the blood money and to whomsoever I pay the blood money, then *I am the recompense for the blood money*" (my italics). The entire allegory of *Conference of the Birds* can be interpreted as a naked and unsentimental extended gloss on this hadith and an unfolding of its rhythms of Discovery, Annihilation, and Resurrection in Divine Identity and Truth. What Mohammed's astonishing hadith makes clear and what *Conference of the Birds* illustrates is that the Path to Unity involves nothing less than a total purification of the false self (called, in Sufi terminology, the *nafs*) by means of a plunging into the abyss of divine passion and revelation that prepares and makes possible a Death into Eternal Life. This is not a Path for the faint-hearted or the lazy or for those who "want to feel good about themselves." It is only for those who have allowed themselves to become both desperate and impassioned enough to risk total transformation. Al-Hallaj wrote, "Between me and You there is only me / Take away the me, so only You remain." The true Sufi path—the one Attar embodies and celebrates in the *Manteq-ut-tair*—faces, without any mask, the rigor and fury of what it means to "take away the me." In its disciplines, three related truths are stressed with tremendous urgency: the necessity of always remembering the unutterable glory, power and majesty of God; the necessity of risking one's entire self in the flame of vast longing and sacred passion; and the necessity of a more and more absolute surrender to the will of the Divine. The rigorous fusion of these three fierce truths leads to that Annihilation (*fana*) of the false self that alone can allow for the full, all-embracing outrageous splendor of the Divine self to break out finally and claim the whole personality.

Attar reveals the depth of his assent to this severe, uncompromising path in his description of the "seven valleys" and in his unfolding of the events that lead to the Simurg's final self-revelation. In his description of the very first valley—the Quest—Attar writes, "You will have to remain for several years in the valley and advance with great patience and perseverance. You will have to perform arduous tasks and to purify your nature. You will have to give up your riches and renounce all you have." Later, when he describes the Valley of Love, Attar tells us with almost brutal candor: "If he who enters on the spiritual path is not wholly consumed by the fire of love, how can he withstand the sadness that will overwhelm him? So long as you do not consume yourself entirely, how can you hope to be free from sorrow?" There are austere laws to spiritual evolution, and Attar is not afraid to state them baldly. In his painstaking, searing accounts of what has to unfold in the last five "valleys"—of Knowledge, Independence and Detachment, Unity, Bewilderment and Stupefaction, Poverty and Annihilation—Attar distills and crystallizes hundreds of years of Sufi esoteric teaching and the inner experience of the lonely and devastating higher reaches of the Path where the false self is systematically—and with a precise, glorious, and terrible ruthlessness—unnerved, undone, and, finally, annihilated altogether. Attar's descriptions have the purity of a theorem in mathematics; he knows the truth of these laws of the Alchemy of Love and Unity too well to dare to mitigate their severity. To do so would be to mislead those seekers who really wanted (and want) the full truth of what the Path and its transformations demand.

This stark candor darkens and deepens in the last pages of the poem. Only thirty of the millions of birds that set out on the journey actually finish it. As Attar writes, "Several died on the way; others again sacrificed their souls on the summit of the mountains; several were roasted by the heat of the sun . . . others went mad and committed suicide . . . some lagged behind disabled by fatigue or wounds; others could not move forward, dazed by the wonders and mysteries of the Path. Some were enchanted by the changing scenery and began to enjoy themselves, forgetting that they were out in quest of the Simurg." The thirty birds that did manage to cross the seven valleys are described as "weary and worn," "without feathers, without hair, full of pain and agony," "heart-broken" and "soul-stricken."

And there are still, even at this late stage, further ordeals the thirty birds have to undergo if they are going to be able to be "killed" completely and given by the Divine the "blood money" of Its own Identity. The first ordeal is in the form of one ultimate test. When the birds tell the Honorable Usher of the Royal Court why they have come, he replies scornfully, "Whether you exist or do not exist is immaterial to the sovereign of Eternity. Millions of worlds filled with a myriad of creatures are like an ant at the door of the King. What then will your place be before Him? Better return, O handful of pilgrims."

This is a terrible and brilliant passage; what the Usher's merciless response actually makes possible for the birds is a crucial, and penultimate, purification—that of any lingering pride they still may have in their achievement of gnosis or endurance and of any secret belief they may still be entertaining of the glory and worth of their search. By the radiant abjection of their reply—"Will the great King reject us with contempt upon this road? Can such an insult proceed from Him, and if it does, will it not turn into honor?"—the birds show the depth of their surrender to the Divine, and the extent of their hopeless freedom from any claim to "reward" for everything that they have endured.

This profound and humble surrender and freedom, Attar tells us, are rewarded by one last, and finally devastating, ordeal: "A register was placed before them, in which every detail of the deeds that each one of them had done, or had omitted to do, from the beginning to the end, was carefully entered."

By this stage of the poem, Attar's ruthlessness with us and his surviving thirty birds is almost unendurable; yet what it reveals is the brilliance of divine mercy and the extreme paradoxical intelligence of the Alchemy of Unity. If every conceivable trace of the false self, the purely human, is not finally destroyed (and what more powerful way of destroying it with birds could be imagined than by presenting those on the threshold of Illumination with a list of everything they have done wrong or omitted to do?), then the complete power and glory of the Divine Soul cannot be unfolded in them and the final premise of Allah as revealed in Mohammed's *hadith* cannot be fulfilled: "Whomsoever I kill, then I must pay the blood money and to whomsoever I owe the blood money then I am the recompense for the blood money."

Finally destroyed, and finally resurrected in Divine Truth and Life, the thirty birds can at last receive the full "recompense" owed them. It is this sublime and awe-inspiring "recompense" that ends the poem in a burst of calm, prolonged ecstasy. "Look where they would, it was only the Simurg they saw." Those who go all the way to the end of the Quest into the Sun of their authentic divine Identity all tell us—whatever tradition they belong to—that all the trials and sufferings of the Way pale before the splendor of what is revealed at the end, and the endless peace, bliss, power, and knowledge that flow effortlessly from that splendor. It is Attar's crowning achievement that he makes us feel that such glory completely and finally repays the birds for everything they have endured—and will repay us also when we find the courage, mad love, and abandoned humility to follow them through Annihilation into Eternal Life.

TRANSLATOR'S FOREWORD

Farid-Ud-Din Attar occupies a prominent place in the roll of distinguished Persian poets. His most famous work on Sufism, written eight centuries ago, is the *Mantiq-ut-Tayr*, or the "Colloquy of the Birds," an allegorical poem in which the gifted mystic describes the quest of the Birds (symbolizing Sufi pilgrims) for the Simurg (the Lord of Creation). A French translation of this great classic by M. Garcin de Tassy was published in Paris in the year 1863, but it has not yet been translated into English. In the year 1910 a translation of a fragment of the poem, in which the poet describes the seven valleys through which the Sufi pilgrim has to make his way before he reaches the Divine presence, appeared in "The Porch," and was subsequently issued in leaflet form. This excerpt, however, gives no idea of the story, nor of the poet's flights of fancy and the charming imagery that distinguish his poem from all other Sufi works. I was eagerly awaiting a full translation of the poem by one of those English scholars who have rendered such splendid service to the cause of oriental studies by bringing within the reach of the English-speaking people many a gem of Persian literature, but as no such work has appeared and as I had a little leisure during my last voyage from Bombay to Venice, I thought I could apply it to no better purpose than the preparation of an abridged version of this great poem, which, dealing with a subject of perennial interest to mankind, has delighted and inspired successive generations of readers and will continue to do so, as long as divine philosophy kindles in the heart of men the fire of enthusiasm to rise on "stepping stones of their dead selves to higher things."

I should explain that I have omitted a good deal which I thought would not interest a foreign reader or would tend to obscure rather than illuminate the salient points of the discourse. I have also thought fit to give a free rather than literal translation of the selected passages, so that the work may be of interest to the casual reader as well as to the student of spiritual and mystic lore.

In these days of restless struggle and haste when the thoughts of men are directed towards a practical solution of the bewildering difficulties into which the world has been plunged by the great war, a work on a system of philosophy identified with metaphysical speculation and stagnation calls for a word of explanation, if not of apology. The highest intelligences in all parts of the globe are to-day striving to gain a clear understanding of the terrible unrest that has everywhere unhinged the minds of the people and to devise means for combating the forces of disruption that threaten to overturn the established order of things. The crying need of the hour is virile action, not sterile speculation. We want powerful stimulants to rouse up every individual to do his best for the regeneration of the world, not soothing drafts to induce the slumber of spiritualism and quietism.

What, then, is the justification for a book on Sufism in such stirring times? The justification lies in the fact that mysticism like other systems of religious philosophy has an ideal as well as a practical side. If it leads some to passivity, or lures them to the realms of fancy, it also quickens others to rise above the plane of common life and come in closer touch with the reality of things. The exalted doctrines and high principles for which it stands sustain alike those who long for a life of spiritual peace and those who are ready to face the stern struggles of an active life. Worthless, indeed, would be these tenets and precepts for the ascent of man should they break down when subjected to the pressure of events such as those through which society is now passing.

Self-renunciation is the be-all and end-all of Sufism, but it must not be confounded with renunciation of the world. Sufism does not call upon its initiates to leave the world. It rather exhorts them to plunge themselves in it and in the universe at their gates and to know their mutual relations. This knowledge cannot come from without by comprehension. It can only be attained from within by self-mergence. Therefore, the Sufi has to go through certain stages of training and preparation. The vital principle of this self-discipline is the purification of the senses and of the will. To purify the senses is to liberate them from the thraldom of egocentric judgment and to make them organs of clear and unclouded perception. This done, the Sufi's heart becomes a mirror on which the full perfection of Divinity can be reflected. The traveler on the Path then energizes upon new planes where he sees more clearly, hears more intensely and feels more vividly than before. After this it is not a very difficult matter for him to surrender his "I-hood" and to subjugate his affections and will. He is now the *Sikandar* (Alexander) of his time, for he has built a solid wall between his pure self and the Gog and Magog of passions and desires. He feels that the rhythm of his life is in tune with the rhythm of the Universal Life, beholds the world from a new angle of vision and discerns the eternal beauty and eternal serenity beneath apparent deformity and apparent inhumanity. The dreadful phantoms of passion and prejudice, distrust and discord vanish like mists and new light, new colour, new fragrance, new music thrill every nerve with indescribable joy.

During his journey on the spiritual path a Sufi is apt to lose self-control and to indulge in excesses. Many an ardent pilgrim has gone astray owing to such loss of control, but that is no reason why others should fight shy of the pilgrimage. If some enthusiasts have brought ridicule on themselves and on the cause by pushing the doctrines of abstinence, love and charity to excess, they have at least left to humanity a warning against the perils of the modern tendency towards a preponderance of the opposite qualities of worldliness, selfishness and self-indulgence. A study of Sufism will thus help us in this materialistic age to steer clear of the arid rocks of egotism while avoiding the engulfing whirlpools of nihilism. The world would indeed be at all times much the better for a little infusion of the exalted devotion of mystics like Mirabai or Muktabai, or of the quietism of Rabi'ah or Madame Guyon, or the transcendentalism of Maulana Rumi or Schelling, or the ecstatic exultation of Mansur Hallaj or Master Eckhart, or of the mystical compulsion of Joan of Arc or Florence Nightingale.

Another aspect of the study of mysticism should not be lost sight of. There is no branch of Oriental or European thought the study of which promotes a better understanding between East and West than mysticism. It removes many a veil of separation that keeps the different races apart from one another and therefore also apart from God, and makes them realize their essential unity beneath superficial diversity. It may be hoped, therefore, that a deeper and more widespread knowledge of the attractive philosophy and lofty ideals of Sufism, which is at once the religious philosophy and popular religion of Islam, will not fail to induce that spirit of love and charity which neither fears nor loathes as alien communities of different colour or creed, but knits them in closer bonds of union as sons of the same family and sharers of the same destiny.

Before I conclude, it is my pleasant duty to express my obligations to those to whom I am indebted for this excursion into Sufi philosophy. It revives grateful memories of the late Professor Mirza Hairat of the Elphinstone College, Bombay—poet, scholar and philosopher—at whose feet I took my first lessons in Sufism. My warm acknowledgments are also due to those Persian and English authors whose works have been my constant companions on the mystic path, particularly to Mr. E. R. Whinfield and Dr. Reynold Nicholson. In giving illustrations from the works of Maulana Rumi, Jami, Shabistari and Hajwari, I have freely availed myself of the excellent English translation of their writings by these learned authors and my readers will, no doubt, agree that I could not have done better.

R. P. MASANI
15th June 1923

PART ONE

The Parliament of the Birds

THE PARLIAMENT OF THE BIRDS

O nce upon a time, in the dim old days, all the birds of the world assembled in solemn conclave to consider a momentous question.

Ever since the dawn of Creation the inhabitants of every city had had a king or leader, called *Shahryar*, or the friend of the city, but these feathered souls had no king to befriend them. Theirs was an army without a general—a position most precarious. How could they be successful in the battle of life without a leader to guide the weak-winged party through the perils of earthly existence? Many an eloquent speaker addressed the assembly, deploring their helpless plight in plaintive terms, bringing tears to the eyes of the tiny ones, and it was unanimously agreed that it was highly desirable, nay, absolutely necessary, that they should place themselves without delay under the protection of a king.

At this stage, full of fervour, leapt forward the Hoopoe (Hud-hud) renowned in the Muslim scriptures for the part she had played as King Solomon's trusted emissary to Bilqis, the Queen of Sheba. She had on her bosom the crest symbolizing her spiritual knowledge and on her head shone the crown of faith.

"Dear birds," she said, "I have the honour to belong to the Celestial Army. I know the Lord and the secrets of creation. When one carries, as I do, the name of God writ large upon its beak, one may be given the credit of knowing many a secret of the spiritual world."

In the same vein of exultation she recounted her physical and mental qualities. She had the gift of divining underground sources of water and had directed the genii to them by pecking the earth. She had gone round the globe in the days of the Deluge and had accompanied Solomon in his journey through dales and deserts. She was the forerunner of his army and his faithful messenger.

"We have a king, my friends," said she, "I have obtained an indication of His court; but to go alone in quest of Him is beyond my power. If however, you accompany me, I think we may hope to reach the threshold of His Majesty. Yea, any friends, we have a king, whose name is Simurg[1], and whose residence is behind Mount Caucasus. He is close by, but we are far away from Him. The road to His throne is bestrewn with obstructions; more than a hundred thousand veils of light and darkness screen the throne. Hundreds of thousands of souls burn with an ardent passion to see Him, but no one is able to find his way to Him. Yet none can afford to do without Him. Supreme manliness, absolute fearlessness and complete self-effacement are needed to overcome those obstacles. If we succeed in getting a glimpse of His face, it will be an achievement indeed. If we do not attempt it, and if we fail to greet the Beloved, this life is not worth living."

The Hoopoe then described to her winged friends how the Simurg had first made His appearance on earth.

"During the early days of Creation He passed one midnight in His radiant flight over the land of China. A feather from His wing fell on Chinese soil. Instantly there was great tumult throughout the world. Everyone was seized with a desire to take a picture of that feather, and whoever saw the picture lost his senses. That feather is still in China's picture-gallery. 'Seek knowledge, even in China' points to this."[2]

On hearing this account of the Simurg, the birds lost all patience and were seized with a longing to set out at once in quest of the Sovereign Bird. They became His friends and their own enemies and wished to go forward in search of Him, but when they were told how long and fearful the road was, they were completely unnerved and brought forward several excuses. These apologies were typical of the personal idiosyncrasies of the different species of the birds.

The first to retrace its steps was the Nightingale, known for his passionate fancy for the Rose and for the rapturous melodies in which he sings of his love. "I am so completely drowned in the ocean of love for my Rose," said he, "that I have practically no life of my own. How can a tiny thing like me have the fortitude to withstand the splendour of the Simurg? For me the love of the Rose is enough."

"Oh," cried the Hoopoe, "ye who stop short at mere appearances, being enamoured of external beauty only, talk no more of Love. Your love for the Rose has merely spread thorns in your way. Such a passion for transient objects brings naught save grief. Give up your fancy for the Rose. It mocks you at every spring and blossoms not for your sake. Your attachment for it is like that of the Dervish in the story I will relate to you."

The Princess and the Dervish

A charming princess was the object of universal admiration. One day an ill-starred *Dervish* (mendicant) happened to pass by. He was so struck with her beauty that the piece of bread he was carrying in his hands slipped from his fingers. Greatly amused, the girl burst into laughter and walked off merrily. The *Dervish* was, however, so much enamoured of her smile, scornful though it was, that he could thenceforth think of nothing else but that smile. For seven long years he refused to move from the precincts of her palace. The attendants and servants of the girl were so much annoyed with him that they resolved one day to take his life. The princess, however, did not wish that the unfortunate man should be injured in any way. She, therefore, whispered to him in secret that if he wished to save his life, he had better leave the place forthwith.

"Have I a life that I should think of saving it?" asked the love-sick man. "On the very day on which you favoured me with a smile, my life was sacrificed to you. But pray, tell me why did you smile that day?"

"Oh, you simpleton," replied the girl. "I laughed because I saw that you had not an iota of sense or reason."

After the Nightingale had been thus admonished by the Hoopoe, the Parrot came forward and pleaded his inability to undertake the journey because he had been imprisoned in a cage, a penalty he had to pay for his beauty. The Peacock urged that he was quite unworthy of the Royal Presence because of the part he had played in the expulsion of Adam from Paradise. The Duck could not do without water, nor the Partridge without mountains. The Huma said he was gifted with the power to confer sovereignty on those over whose head he flew. Why should he give up such a lofty privilege? Similarly, the Falcon could not brook the idea of relinquishing his place of honour on the hand of kings. The Heron wished to stay in the lagoons, and the Owl in the ruins of which he was the undisturbed monarch. Last came the Wagtail with his excuses for his weakness and physical disabilities that made it impossible for him to embark on the journey.[3]

The Hoopoe brushed aside all these pretexts and illustrated her precepts by a series of anecdotes and inspiring stories; for instance, in admonishing the Owl, she related the following story, illustrating the fate of those who, like the Owl, are attached to their worldly possessions.

A Miser's Fate

A miser died, leaving a pot full of coins, buried in a secret place. Some time after his death, his son saw him in a dream. His appearance was completely metamorphosed, so that he looked like a mouse, and streams of tears were flowing from his eyes. In this state of agony he was going round and round the place where the treasure lay buried. "My sire," asked the son, "what has transformed your features thus? Wherefore this deformity?"

"Whosoever's heart is so attached to riches as was mine," replied the father, "will have his face deformed like mine. Therefore, beware, my son. Take a lesson from this."

Sage counsel such as this had its effect. The Hoopoe's words instilled courage and enthusiasm into the hearts of the birds, and they resolved to embark on the journey, perilous though it was. Before starting, however, they asked her to expound to them their relationship with His Majesty the Simurg, a point that was by no means clear to them.

"Know ye then," said the Hoopoe, "that the Simurg once removed the veil from His face, so that it shone resplendent like the sun and cast millions of rays around. By his grace, these rays were turned into birds. We are, therefore, the sparks of the Simurg. When you realize this mystery, your relationship with the Simurg will be as clear to you as day-light. But, beware, my friends, do not reveal this secret to others. It is not a matter to be divulged to all. Well, now that you have learnt whose reflection or shadow you are, you will understand that to live or to die is one and the same thing for you."

This, however, was a metaphysical subtlety too difficult for the bewildered birds to comprehend. The Hoopoe, therefore, gave an illustration.

A Handsome King

There was a king, handsome above all other men. His subjects' great desire was to behold his face. Those who merely thought of his beauty lost their senses, while those who succeeded in getting a glimpse of the Royal Presence forthwith gave up their lives. Thus, neither could they endure the sight, nor could they do without it. Out of compassion for them, the king arranged to show his face to them through a mirror, so as to protect them from exposure to the overpowering rays of his beauty. A special palace was, therefore, erected for the purpose, and a mirror was placed in front of it in such a position that if the king turned his face in a particular direction, people were able to see its reflection in the mirror.[4]

"If you, my friends," continued the Hoopoe, "desire to see the face of our beloved king Simurg, I will tell you where to look for it. In the mirror of your own heart you will be able to see Him."

This again fired the hearts of the birds with the desire to greet the Simurg. They unanimously resolved to set out in quest of the Great Unknown. At the same time they could not help doubting their capacity to withstand the perils of the journey. Seeing the perturbed state of their mind, the Hoopoe said: "He who has become a lover should never think of his life. Your soul is an obstacle in your way. Sacrifice it. If you are required to sacrifice your faith also, together with your soul, do so by all means, and if anyone brands you as an infidel, tell him that love occupies a position more exalted than religion, and has nothing to do with faith or heresy. Whoever sets his feet firmly in the abiding-place of love I transcends the bounds of infidelity and faith as well."

As an illustration of this rather astounding statement, the Hoopoe related to the birds the following.

Story of Shaykh San'an

Shaykh San'an was a saint renowned in Mecca for his devotion and austerities and for his unique knowledge of Sufism. For fifty years he was the acknowledged leader of the learned men of Mecca, and the distinguished preceptor of hundreds of disciples. Such was his personal purity and such were his natural gifts for performing miracles that a single breath of his was sufficient to cure the worst of maladies. For several successive nights this saint saw in a dream that he had gone from Mecca to Byzantium and was there prostrating himself before an idol. He thereupon told his disciples that be apprehended that a serious calamity was awaiting him and that rather than remain in suspense he proposed to proceed to Byzantium in order to obtain a clue to the interpretation of that dream. All his followers, four hundred in number, accompanied him. When they reached their destination they came to a palace, on the tower of which stood a Christian girl. She was endowed with celestial beauty and angelic qualities, and was well versed in spiritual knowledge. On seeing her face, the Shaykh stood riveted to the ground and lost all that was his. His followers felt greatly embarrassed, but ventured to proffer their advice to their erstwhile teacher and leader, and even to remonstrate with him for this loss of self-control. Nothing, however, could restore the saint to his senses. They, therefore, did their best to induce him to return to Mecca, but the Shaykh would not budge an inch. He made that street his residence and, mixing with the curs of the street, lived the life of a dog. Misery and illness reduced him to a skeleton, and his saintliness and splendour gave way to infidelity and infamy.

The girl at last came to know of this tragedy. One day she went to the Shaykh and asked, "O holy man, what is the reason for this restlessness and misery? What is the explanation for this strange phenomenon that a pious Muslim should take up his abode in the streets of infidels such as Christians are?"

"You have stolen my heart," said the saint. "Either restore it to me, or accept my love. This love is no mere fancy. Either separate my heart from my body, or lower your head towards mine."

"You should be ashamed of yourself, old fool," said the girl. "At this stage of your life you had better think of your coffin rather than of love for a girl like me.

"Abuse me as much as you may," replied the Shaykh. "That will not affect in the least my attachment to you. Alike are old and young in the path of love. Its impress on the heart of all is the same."

"If that is so," observed the girl, "and if your love is genuine, you must wash your hands clean of Islam. The fancy of one who observes diversity of creed in the realm of love is no more enduring then mere colour (appearance) and smell."

"I am prepared to do whatever you desire and shall perform with all my heart whatever you dictate."

"Then," said the girl, "do these things: prostrate yourself before an idol; put the Quran in the fire; drink wine and renounce Islam."

The bewildered Shaykh replied: "I can go so far as to persuade myself to drink wine in honour of your beauty, but the other things I can never do."

"Very well," said the girl, "come and drink wine?"

To a temple they repaired, where the Shaykh saw a novel assemblage of persons, presided over by a fascinating hostess. Glowing with passion, he took goblet after goblet from the hand of his beloved and lost all sense and reason and attempted to take her in his arms.

"Not yet," said the girl, "you are still a pretender in the path of love. If your attachment is real and firm, follow my ringlets[5] in heresy and become a Christian."

The drunken Sufi adopted Christianity.

"Now what more do you want?" he asked. "In my senses I declined to prostrate before an idol, but in this intoxicated condition I have become a worshipper of an idol such as you."

"You want to be one with me," replied the girl, "but I am a princess. I must have a dowry befitting a princess. Where will you find so much gold and silver? Therefore, take my advice. Recover your senses, forget this passion; be a man, and have patience like a man."

Mortally disappointed, the Shaykh implored her not to be unkind. It was impossible for him, at that stage to do without her.

"Well then," said the girl, "watch my herd of pigs for a year and I will forego the dowry."

What a position for a Muslim saint, whose religion holds the pig to be the most unclean animal! Yet the infatuated man agreed at once.[6]

The Shaykh's disciples returned to Mecca, greatly mortified by the conduct of the God-forsaken saint. They dared not show their faces in public. When they had left for Byzantium, the most devoted disciple of the Shaykh was not in Mecca. He was not, therefore, able to accompany his colleagues, but when he heard from them of the condition to which the Shaykh was reduced, he took them all to task for their inactivity and inconstancy.

"You should have all turned Christians and remained with the Shaykh rather than have deserted him," said he.

"We were prepared to do even that," they replied, "but the Shaykh would not allow us to do so, and he bade us return home."

"In that case," observed the disciple, "you should have knocked unceasingly at the door of the Almighty for his redemption."

Thereupon, they all forthwith proceeded to Byzantium, retired to a sequestered place and for forty days and nights unceasingly offered prayers for the salvation of the holy man. During this interval they touched neither food nor water, nor rested for a moment.

On the dawn following the fortieth night, when the faithful disciple was engaged in his morning prayers, he felt an exquisitely delightful breeze blowing in the direction in which he was standing. The veil before the world was lifted and he saw His Holiness; the Prophet of Islam, approaching him.

The disciple fell on his knees at once and said: "Our Shaykh has lost the way. We beseech you to show him the way."

"O man of supreme courage and lofty spirit," said the Prophet, "let your soul abide in peace. Your leader has been set free from imprisonment. This achievement is due to your magnanimity and earnest efforts. A cloud of dust had arisen between the Shaykh and the Lord Almighty. I have removed it. He is no longer grovelling in darkness, but is now penitent and implores forgiveness for his sins. Rest assured, such is the virtue of penitence that a hundred worlds of sinfulness, standing as an impenetrable barrier between man and his Creator, disappear with a single breath of sincere repentance."

On hearing this, the disciple was filled with delight. He raised a cry of joy and informed his colleagues of the glad tidings.

They started immediately in search of the Shaykh and found him engaged in prayer, radiant as fire and happy in his supplications. On beholding his disciples, he wept most bitterly, tore his garments into tatters and covered his head with dust. His followers said: "O Shaykh, now is the time for thanksgiving, not for lamentation. The night of sorrow has passed; the morn of hope has dawned."

They then related to him how the Prophet had vouchsafed his grace to him, and had bid him be of good cheer for henceforth he was sure to find his way to the Creator in a better light. The Shaykh thereupon put on his *khirka* (Sufi garment), and returned to Mecca.

The story, however, does not end there. The curtain now rises over a novel scene. It is now the turn of the girl to see a dream. She sees the vision of the Sun dropping by her side. In miraculous tones the Sun thus spoke to her: "Go after the Shaykh immediately. Adopt his faith and be the dust of his feet. Aye, thou that polluteth him, be pure by his grace. He had not set foot in thy path intentionally and deliberately to win thy love, but thou must go to him with a set purpose. Thou didst mislead him and turn him from the right path. Therefore, be his companion now and go his way. How long wilt thou remain in ignorance? Seek divine knowledge from him and acquire proficiency in the philosophy of Love through him."

The girl awoke from this reverie, profoundly stirred. She commenced weeping and lamenting and set out in search of the saint, not pausing for a moment to think who would point her the way out of the wilderness and give a clue to the whereabouts of the Shaykh. In her grief and supplication to the Almighty, she cried: "O Thou who knowest the truth, it is true that I made thy devotee lose the Path, but I was ignorant. Punish me not for my folly. Forgive me for all that happened for me and through me."

About the same time the Shaykh had a message from the Unseen World that the girl had abandoned Christianity, and that she should be admitted to the faith of Islam. "Turn back, therefore, and go once more in search of that idol of yours. Be one with her in thought and knowledge."

The Shaykh proceeded forthwith in quest of the girl and once more there was great consternation in the camp of his disciples.

"Oh Shaykh," they expostulated, "is this the end of all your penitence and mortification? Whence again this infatuation?"

The Shaykh, however, explained to them what had happened, and they all set out in search of the girl. They found her lying on the ground, bare-headed, bare-footed, wrapped in tatters, and quite insensible. They managed to restore her to her senses, but on seeing the Shaykh, she fell into a swoon. When she recovered her senses, she implored him to initiate her into the faith of Islam. The Shaykh chanted the words of the Quran in her ears. She became restless after this conversion and she felt that the moment of bidding farewell to this world of trial and humiliations had arrived. "Forgive me, O Shaykh," she muttered, and with those words the sun of her existence concealed itself behind the cloud of non-existence. She was a drop of the Ocean of Truth and was merged in the Ocean again.

After the death of the girl, the Shaykh told his pupils that it was impossible for him to live any longer, and he also breathed his last the same day. He was buried by the side of the girl's grave, and from it there sprang up a fountain of pure, transparent water; it keeps the spot green with verdure throughout the year; and is therefore a place of pilgrimage for people coming from the four corners of the world.[7]

When the birds heard this love-story from the lips of the Hoopoe, the flame of their love for the Simurg was rekindled in their hearts a thousandfold. They now cared not for their lives and resolved to set out in search of the Beloved. They had, however, no leader, and a leader was indispensable for such a difficult journey. It was, therefore, decided to determine by lot who should be their guide. Fortunately for them, the honour fell to the lot of the worthiest of them all, and that was the Hoopoe. All of them took an oath of allegiance to her, and they placed a crown upon her head.

PART TWO

"On to the Bound of the Waste, On, to the City of God"

"ON TO THE BOUND OF THE WASTE, ON, TO THE CITY OF GOD"

The march now commenced. The road was, however, so fearful that after they had proceeded a short distance, every one of them began to tremble. They, therefore, halted at a convenient spot. They had serious misgivings as to the result of their adventure, and they felt that unless their doubts and difficulties were overcome, it would be impossible to proceed further. They, therefore, requested the Hoopoe to sit on a throne and answer the questions they wished to put to her. The Hoopoe accordingly took her seat on the royal throne.

A bird then came forward and said to the Hoopoe: "You are just like ourselves, and we are just like you. Nevertheless, you are far ahead of us in the path of the Truth. Why this difference?"

"This blessing is due to the fact that I had a glance from Solomon for a moment," said she. "This position has not been attained by mere devotion and service, or by spending silver and gold. All this good fortune is a result of a favorable glance. You should also spend your life in devotion and await the grace of Solomon. As soon as that grace is vouchsafed to you, you will rise higher than any stage that I can describe to you."

Sultan Mahmud and the Orphan Lad

One day Sultan Mahmud wandered away from his retinue, and saw a boy seated on the bank of a river with a fishing-rod. He had a pale and haggard look.

"Why so pale and sad, little one?" asked Mahmud. "Sir," said the boy, "we are seven children. Our father is dead and our mother infirm and bed-ridden. She has not a penny to buy food for us. During the day I try to catch fish, and that forms our meal in the evening."

The king asked for the rod, and offered to give half the spoil to him. The boy consented. Princely fortune now favoured the orphan. They had a haul of a hundred fish that day. The boy wondered what the reason for such extraordinary good luck could be and offered the king half the share of the fish. He, however, bade the lad keep the whole. The next day he sent for the boy and said, "Come now, yesterday we were partners in the fishing enterprise; now I want you to be a partner in my kingdom."

No sooner said than done. Mahmud made over half his territories to the lad. An old acquaintance asked the boy how he had managed to attain that position. "My grief was turned into joy," said he, "because a fortunate man happened to pass by me."

Another bird then submitted that he was very weak, whereas the road was far away and full of obstacles. "In the very first stage of the journey I shall succumb," he said. "Where the most gallant and valiant souls have fallen and are lying in eternal sleep, I can only raise a little dust and shall be for ever lost."

"Know thou," said the Hoopoe, "this world is a den of impurities. Why set your heart on it? Why fear death? Each one of us has to die some day. So long as a man is not completely dead to his own self and to the world, his soul does not enter the realms of purity. Therefore, do not, like a woman, bring fresh excuses. Once divine love penetrates the heart of a man, it makes him as brave as a lion, even though he may be as feeble as an ant. How can one who takes a leap into the ocean of adventure accept any drink but the blood of his heart?"

Another bird said, "I am a sinner. Who would admit such an unworthy creature into the presence of the Simurg?"

"Oh benighted one," replied the Hoopoe, "do not despair. Lower your head in penitence. Pray for divine mercy. If you repent with a sincere heart, you will obtain a thousand keys to open the gate to that path of Divinity. The grace of providence transcends our comprehension."[8]

"I am a creature of a vacillating disposition," observed another bird, "at times saintly in thought, at times sinful. Sometimes, I am beside myself in a tavern; sometimes lost in prayer and meditation. At times Satan drags me away from the path of righteousness; at times angels guide and restore me to that path. Such is my pitiful condition."

"Listen to me, you perplexed creature," said the Hoopoe. "Such is the condition of all in creation. If one would not trip, one would not lower his head in penitence. If all were godly, would there be any room for the prophets?"

Another bird submitted: "My passion is my enemy. This dog of passion never cares for my inclinations and instructions. I know not how to make him subservient to my will."

"This world abounds in millions of slaves of this dog," said the Hoopoe. "He leads them all by the nose. Thousands of these slaves die in disgrace, but this infidel of a dog never dies. Listen to this story."

A Grave-Digger's Experience

A man grew grey in the work of digging graves.

"You have spent all your life in excavating the earth," said a man to him. "Pray tell me, did you discover any mystery under the bowels of this earth?"

"I have seen this mystery," he replied. "For three score years and ten the dog of my passion[9] saw me incessantly digging graves for frail mortals, but the constant sight of the spectre of death and of heart-rending funerals has not produced the slightest impression on him. He has not been dead or dormant for a moment. Not once has he obeyed the call of reason, not once has he offered a prayer."

Shah Abbas once remarked, "It is possible that myriads of infidels in this world will some day adopt the true faith, but although a hundred thousand and twenty prophets have been sent into this world, so that this faithless dog of passion may either become a Musalman or be annihilated, none has hitherto succeeded in accomplishing either of the two missions. Under the sway of passion we are all infidels. We have been harbouring an infidel in our own hearts. To destroy that infidel is no easy matter, but he is a true hero who chases him and puts fetters round his hands and feet, and a chain about his neck. The dust under the feet of such a man is infinitely more precious than the blood of others."

Another bird complained, "I am waylaid by Satan *(Iblis)*. He haunts me, even while I am engaged in prayers. Tell me how I may be saved from his snares."

"So long as the dog of passion runs in front of you," replied the Hoopoe, "so long will Iblis seize you by the throat.[10] Your own desires are your Satan. Subservience to this devil turns this earth into a hell. A foolish man once complained to a Sufi saint that Satan had seduced and waylaid him and had made him miserable. The Sufi told him that Satan had been there only a minute before and had lodged a complaint against the man himself. "What Satan told me," said the saint, "was this: 'My jurisdiction extends over the whole world. I have nothing to do with those who withdraw themselves from my domain. Therefore, tell this man to tread in the Path of God, and to wash his hands of the earth. Whoever keeps away from my province has no reason to fear me. Farewell.'"

"I am in love with gold," said another bird. "My desire for wealth is so great that it stands like an idol in my way."

"It is but coloured tinsel," replied the Hoopoe. "You have taken a fancy for it just as a child is enamoured of coloured baubles. Give up such childish fancies, and scatter in all directions whatever you have got. I will tell you a story that will perhaps inspire you to do so."

A Saint's Dream

A holy man saw in a dream that while he was walking in the path of Truth an angel accosted him.

"Whither are you going?" asked the angel.

"I am on my way to the Royal Presence," was the reply.

"You are engaged in so many worldly affairs," said the angel. "You have taken such a lot of baggage with you, so much wealth and property. How can you hope to be admitted to the Royal Presence with all this paraphernalia?"

"The saint thereupon threw away all the baggage he had, and kept with him only a piece of blanket to protect him from inclement weather and serve as a garment. The next night he saw the angel again in a dream.

"Well, where are you going to-day?"

"To the seat of the Lord of Creation."

"O man of wisdom," said the angel, "how can you get there with this piece of blanket? It is a terrible obstacle in your way."

Waking from his dream, the holy man put the blanket in the fire.

On the third night the saint saw the angel once more.

"O pure liver," said the angel, "whither are you going?"

"I am going to the Creator of the Universe."

"O illustrious man," observed the angel, "now that you have stripped yourself of all that you had, remain where you are. You have no need to go anywhere in search of the Creator. He will Himself come to you."[11]

Another bird then came forward and said: "I love my country. I have my home on the top of a lovely palace. Securely perched upon it, I feel as happy as a king. Why should I take upon myself the worries and the perils of a journey through wastes and wildernesses? Would any wise man give up the pleasures of paradise and prefer the awful toil and travail of such a journey?"

This babble roused the ire of the Hoopoe.

"O mean-spirited, cowardly creature," said be, "are you a dog that you wish to sit on this dung-heap and rot there? Your real palace is in heaven, not on earth. Listen to this story."

A King's Palace

A king had a magnificent palace built for him. When it was completed, he invited all his courtiers and asked them whether any one of them could discover any defect therein. They were all unanimous in declaring that no one had ever before seen such a flawless and stately mansion. A discordant note was, however, struck by a holy man who happened to be present.

"Allow me to say, Your Majesty," said he, "there is an aperture in this palace, which is a serious defect."

"What balderdash is this!" exclaimed the monarch in a rage. "I have never seen any aperture in it anywhere."

"Yes, Your Majesty," replied the sage; "there is a tiny hole, through which *Izrael*, the Angel of Death, will find his way. If you can manage to fill it up, do so. If not, of what use are your palace and your crown and your throne? The mansion now appears to be as beautiful and lovely as paradise itself, but when the Angel of Death knocks at the door, it will be as dreadful and loathsome as hell."

A love-sick bird then came forward. "My love for my beloved is so strong," said he, "that I cannot live for a moment without seeing her face."

"This is a mere fancy," said the Hoopoe. "It is not real love, born of *ma'rifat* or divine knowledge. Cure thy heart of such a morbid desire for appearances."

Another bird represented that he was terribly afraid of death. "I apprehend," said the bird, "that I shall die of fear during the very first stage of the journey."

The Hoopoe replied, "We are all foredoomed to death. Although you may be enjoying sovereignty all your life, you will have to depart one day. Therefore, renounce the world and prepare for the journey to the realm of non-existence. Do not spoil the chances of Eternal Life for the sake of this mean world."

"Not one of my desires has ever been fulfilled," was the plaint of another bird. "I am, therefore, utterly depressed and heart-sick. I do not think I can undertake this journey."

"Gratification and disappointment of desires pertaining to the transient objects of this world are alike illusory," replied the Hoopoe. "He cannot be said to be alive whose heart is attached to transient things. You have therefore no heart, my friend."

Another bird said, "O light of our eyes, I am ready to carry out the behests of the Lord. Whether He accepts my humble services or not, I am prepared to proffer them to Him."

"Well said," replied the Hoopoe. "There can be no better virtue than this. How can you take your soul to Him, if you carry with you your soul (consciousness of self)? You will be able to take your soul to Him, only if you carry out His behests with your soul, surrendering it absolutely to His will."

"Remember," continued the sage mentor, "such devotion and self-sacrifice are very noble, but there should be no trace of irreverence or want of decorum in such service. I will illustrate what I mean by a story. One day a king presented a robe of honour to one of his attendants. The fool wiped his face, which had been covered with dust, with the sleeve of his robe. A man happened to witness this vulgarity and reported the matter to the king. The attendant was at once beheaded."

"Explain to me, please, the mysteries of negation and self-annihilation," said another bird. "I hold it unlawful for me to be absorbed in self. Whatever I touch stings me like a scorpion. I have therefore renounced all things, and it is my earnest prayer that I may be able to have a glimpse of the Royal Presence."

"It is not given to all," said the Hoopoe, "to tread this path. The only provisions for the journey in the Path of Truth are total renunciation and self-annihilation. Consume to ashes whatsoever thou hast."

A Father's Love

An old man in Turkestan had two most beloved objects—his swift-footed horse and his son. "I hold nothing dearer than these two," said the old man, "but if anyone informs me that my son is dead, I would present to that person my favourite horse as a thanksgiving for the good news; because, my friend, I see that these two objects are like two idols in my way."[12]

"Indeed," continued the Hoopoe, "I can think of no better fortune for a valiant man than this that he loses himself from himself."

"O master of foresight," said another bird in great exultation, "although I am frail in body, I carry with me loftiness of spirit in the Path of Truth. Although I cannot boast of much devotion, I can lay claim to more than a little magnanimity."

"Valour alone is the key to the gates of difficulties," observed the Hoopoe. "Whoever possesses a particle of magnanimity eclipses the sun with that small atom. The key to the sovereignty of the world is magnanimity. The wing and feather of the bird of the world is magnanimity. Men of valour cheerfully surrender their soul and body. For years they undergo burning and boiling. The bird of their magnanimity, therefore, approaches the Royal Presence. It passes beyond the region of this world as well as that of faith. If you are not a man of such spirit, move on since you do not belong to the race of the magnanimous."

Shaykh Ahmed Guri and Sultan Sanjar

Shaykh Ahmed Guri was renowned for his gallantry and intrepidity. One day he sought shelter under a bridge with his followers. By chance Sultan Sanjar happened to pass by the bridge.

"What crowd is there under the bridge?" he asked.

"We are without head or foot," said the saint. "If you regard us as your friends, soon shall we strip you of your sovereignty. If, on the other hand, you are our enemy and not our friend, we shall instantly denounce you as an infidel. Think well of our friendship and our enmity. Set your feet in the realm of either and see yourself disgraced."

Sanjar said: "I am not your man. I am neither your friend nor your enemy. I am going away at once so that my harvest may not be burnt."

The Hoopoe sums up the discourse by adding: "Whoever enters the path with a valiant spirit will command respect like a prince, even though he may be a pauper."

Another bird enquired, "What is the value of justice and fidelity in the supreme court of the Simurg? By the grace of God I am treading in the path of justice, and I have never been faithless to anyone."

"The queen of all virtues is justice," said the Hoopoe. "You will obtain a much richer reward if you act with justice than if you devote your whole life to prayer and prostration. There is, moreover, no deed more valiant than an act of justice."

A Faithful Infidel and a Deceitful Crusader

There was a hand to hand fight between a Muhammadan crusader and a high-minded idolater. The Muhammadan asked for a little respite in order to perform his devotions. After the prayer was over, the fight was renewed. It was then time for the "infidel" to offer his prayers. There was another interval in the hostilities. The "infidel," who was more righteous than the crusader, selected a quiet corner, took out his idol and prostrated himself before it. When his adversary saw the face of this idol-worshipper laid on the earth, he said to himself, "This is my opportunity." He was about to unsheathe his sword and cut off the head of his enemy, when he heard a voice from the invisible world: "O treacherous man, faithless from head to foot, how beautifully do you keep your faith and carry out your promise! The idolater showed goodness to you, whereas you contemplate evil. Do unto others as you would do to yourself. From the infidel proceeded fidelity to you. Where is your fidelity, if you are really faithful? O Musulman, you have shown yourself to be a non-Musulman. In the path of faith you have lagged behind an infidel."

These words moved the crusader to tears.

"Why do you weep?" asked his antagonist.

"For your sake I am condemned as an infidel," said the soldier.

The idolater raised a cry when he heard what had happened and he began to shed tears. Deeply impressed with the sublimity of Islam, he embraced that religion and burnt his idol.

The moral is that a man may think that his perfidiousness is hidden from human eyes, but the vault of heaven will expose all his wicked thoughts and deeds one after another and dumfound the sinner.

The Magic Cup of Joseph

When there was famine in Canaan, the brothers of Joseph went to Egypt in the hope of getting some grain from the Governor of the place. Joseph was the Governor and he knew them, but they knew him not. They related to him the story of their misery and prayed for relief. Joseph's face was hidden under a veil and in front of him there was a wonderful cup. He struck his hand on the cup which gave out a mournful tune.

"Can you make out what the cup says?" Joseph asked his brothers.

"O knower of secrets," they replied, "none of us knows what the cup proclaims."

"I know what it says," said Joseph. "It says that you had a brother, handsome beyond description. His name was Joseph and he surpassed you in virtue."

He then struck his fingers on the cup again and said: "The cup says further that you threw him in a pit. You soaked his shirt in the blood of an animal to lend colour to your story that he had been devoured by a wolf. You thus drowned the heart of his bereaved father in blood."

Once more he put his hand on the cup and said: "The cup adds that you consumed the heart of your father and sold your brother. O faithless men, who would display such conduct towards a brother? Shame on you, infidels. By throwing Joseph in a pit, you all placed yourselves in a ditch of woes."

The wicked brothers were thunderstruck. Tears came into their eyes.[13]

A boastful bird said: "I have renounced everything. I am, therefore, worthy of His love so long as I am alive."

"Such bragging and such pretentiousness do not enable one to be a companion of the Simurg on the heights of Kuh-i-kaf," retorted the

Hoopoe. "Do not for a moment boast of your love for Him. What are you? What can you yourself achieve? Whatever takes place proceeds from Him."

"In spite of this rebuke, another irrepressible braggadocio came forward. "I think," said he, "I have acquired perfection. I have also gone through a course of the most difficult austerities and renunciation. Why should I go further than this? My mission in life has already been fulfilled. Is there any one so foolish as he who, seated on treasure, would leave his comfortable seat and go out into wastes and wildernesses in search of treasure?"

"Ah, demon-spirited, conceited fool," exclaimed the Hoopoe, "You have become totally drowned in egotism. The Devil has entered your head. All your perfection and virtues are mere figments of your imagination. As long as you are haunted by such devilish ideas, you will remain far away from the truth. Listen to this story."

The Advice of Satan

One day God Almighty asked Moses to learn some secret from Iblis (Satan). Moses went to Iblis and requested him to teach him a secret. "Remember this one lesson," said Iblis, "Never say 'I'; otherwise you will find yourself in the same condition as I am."[14]

Another bird asked, "What shall we do to keep ourselves cheerful during the journey?"

"Be cheerful," replied the Hoopoe, "with the thought of the existence of the Simurg. He whose heart is set on the Lord never dies. How can the angel of Death venture to approach him!"

"What shall we ask of the Simurg when we meet Him?" asked another bird.

This silly question roused the indignation of the Hoopoe. "Oh ignoramus, why should you ask anything of Him? Ask for Him, and Him alone. Listen to this story."

Sultan Mahmud and Ayaz

One day Sultan Mahmud offered his crown to his favourite slave, Ayaz. All the courtiers were consumed with jealousy. Poor Ayaz began to weep. When he was asked the reason for such grief in the midst of such good fortune, he said, "I have nothing to do with anything but the King. I want him alone, whereas by giving me the crown, he wants to keep me engaged in the affairs of the State and withdraws himself from me. This makes my heart bleed with the thought of separation."

"If you want to know how to adore the Lord," observed the Hoopoe, "learn it from Ayaz."[15]

"What shall we proffer at the feet of the Simurg?" was the question of another bird.

"Take that which is not there," was the reply. "There is enough of wisdom there, and enough of mysteries and Divine Knowledge. There is also no lack of devotion shown by the angels to the Lord. There is, however, no trace in that place of the yearning of the heart and the burning of the soul. Therefore, take these two things there.[16]

"Oh wise guide of ours," cried a bird, "in this wilderness our eyes have grown dim owing to the hardships of the journey. Pray tell us, how many miles still remain to be traversed?"

"We have to cross seven valleys covered with forests," replied the Hoopoe. "After the seventh valley will be discovered the seat of the Simurg. No one can say how many miles it is from this place, because no one who has gone there has ever returned. All those who have entered this road have gone astray for ever. How can you, then, expect any one to give you any information of the path?"

These are the seven valleys:

- The first is the Valley of the Quest.

- The second of Love.

- The third of Knowledge.

- The fourth of Independence and Detachment.

- The fifth of Unity.

- The sixth of Bewilderment and Stupefaction.

- The seventh of Poverty and Annihilation.

PART THREE

Through the Seven Valleys

THE VALLEY OF THE QUEST

As soon as you set your foot in the first valley, that of the Search, thousands of difficulties will assail you unceasingly at every stage. Every moment you will have to go through a hundred tests. The parrot of the sky[17] is only a fly in that place. You will have to remain for several years in the valley, and advance with great patience and perseverance. You will have to perform arduous tasks to purify your nature. You will have to give up your riches and renounce all that you have. When you have attained the certitude that you no longer possess anything, you will still have to detach your heart from all that exists. When your heart is thus rescued from perdition, you will witness the serene light of His Divine Majesty, and when it dawns upon your spirit, your spiritual desires will be multiplied a thousandfold.

On the path of the spiritual traveller there ought to be such a fire of desires that countless new vales will then appear, each one more difficult to cross than the rest. Drawn by the ardour of Love, the enthusiastic pilgrim will plunge into these valleys like a mad man, precipitating himself like a moth into the midst of the flame. Impelled by his zeal, he will give himself up to the quest symbolized by this valley. He will ask the Eternal Cup-Bearer to give him a "draught of the wine." After he has taken a few drops of this wine, he will forget both the worlds. Straight will he be submerged in the Ocean of Immensity; his lips will, nevertheless, be dry with the desire of the quest, and of no one else but his own heart can he demand the secret of eternal beauty. In his longing to know this mystery, he will not be afraid of the dragons that threaten to devour him.

If, at any moment, Faith and Infidelity should be held out to him for a choice, he would seize with alacrity either the one or the other, provided it would show him the path leading to his longed-for goal.

Once the gate is opened, what is faith, and what is infidelity to him? On the other side of the gate there is neither the one nor the other.

Majnun's Search of Layla

One day Majnun was sifting earth in the middle of a road. A pious man said to him: "Oh Majnun, what are you seeking here?"

"I seek Layla," replied Majnun.

"How can you find Layla here?" said the other. "Could a pearl so pure be found in such rubbish?"

"Well" said Majnun, "I seek her everywhere, so that one day I may find her somewhere."

Mahmud and the Rag-Picker

One evening Sultan Mahmud saw a poor man sifting dust in search of some trinkets. Mahmud thereupon threw his diamond wristlet in the heap of dust that the man had collected. Next evening he went to the same place and saw the same man engaged in the same occupation.

"What you obtained yesterday," said the king, who was greatly astonished at the cupidity of the man, "was enough for your maintenance for ten lives, and yet you are grovelling in the dust to-day. Go and enjoy yourself."

"The hidden treasure that I found yesterday," replied the man, "was received from this dust. When fortune smiled on me for knocking at this door, it behoves me that I should devote myself to this work as long as I live."

THE VALLEY OF LOVE

After the first valley, comes the Valley of Love. Whoever sets foot in it, is plunged in fire. Ah, what am I saying? One must oneself be made of fire, otherwise one cannot exist there. The lover, true and sincere, ought, in fact, to be as glowing as fire. His countenance must be radiant with fire, and he must be as ardent and impetuous as a flame of fire.

He must not for a moment think of consequences. He must be ready and willing to fling a hundred worlds into the fire, knowing neither faith nor infidelity, neither doubt nor belief. In this road there is no difference between good and evil. Here neither good nor evil exists. Love transcends both.[18] O thou who liveth unmoved by any cares, this discourse can produce no impression on thee! He, in whose heart sincerity abides, stakes all he has, aye, stakes his head itself, to clasp hands with his beloved. Some are content with the promise of to-morrow that is made to them, but this adept demands it in hard cash. If he who enters upon the spiritual Path is not wholly consumed by the fire of love, how can he withstand the sadness which will overwhelm him? So long as you do not consume yourself entirely, how can you hope to be free from sorrow? A fish, thrown ashore by the ocean, will struggle until he gets back into the water.

In this valley Love is represented by fire, Reason by smoke. When Love bursts into flame, Reason is forthwith dissipated like smoke. Reason cannot coexist with Love's mania, for Love has nothing whatever to do with human Reason. If ever you attain a clear vision of the unseen world, then only will you be able to realize the source of Love. By the odour of Love every atom in the world is intoxicated. It owes its existence to the existence of Love.

If you possessed the spiritual insight to penetrate the invisible world, the atoms of the visible world would also become unveiled to you, but if you regard these with the eye of intellect, you will never comprehend love as you should. Only one who has gone through the test and has become free can feel this spiritual devotion. You have not acquired such experience. You have not even the inspiration of love.[19] You are selfish, dead, so to say, and therefore unworthy of love. He who enters upon this path should have thousands of hearts, fired with devotion, so that every moment he may be able to sacrifice a hundred souls.

A Love-Sick Nobleman

A nobleman had a passion for a young wine-seller. So strong was his attachment that it grew into madness. He left his home and wandered desolate from place to place and the infamy of his life became the subject of gossip far and wide. He sold all that he had and bought wine. When he had nothing left with him, his passion increased a hundredfold. Although he was given as much bread as he desired, he remained always hungry, because he carried off all the bread he received, and bought wine with it. Hungry he always remained, so that he might gulp down in one moment a hundred draughts of wine. One day a man said to him: "O unfortunate man, tell me what is love. Pray, divulge this secret to me."

"Love is this," replied the man, "that thou shouldst sell the merchandise of a hundred worlds to buy wine (the symbol of love). How can a man understand love and its anguish until he has done this?"[20]

Majnun's Stratagem

The family of Layla never allowed Majnun to enter their territory even for a moment. In that desert there was a shepherd. Majnun bought of him a sheep-skin. Bending his head he clad himself in that skin and he looked like a sheep. He then told the shepherd: "For the sake of God, let me join the fold of your sheep. Drive the sheep to Layla's dwelling and let me be in the midst so that I may have a glimpse of her face for a moment. Thus Majnun found his way to his beloved. The sight of Layla at first filled his heart with joy, but after a while he fell down unconscious. The shepherd took him to the plains, threw water on his face and brought him to his senses. After this Majnun was sitting one day in the desert with the shepherds when one of his countrymen saw him and said: "O man of respectable lineage, why art thou without clothing? If thou wilt permit me, I will forthwith bring for thee the garment that thou dost most desire." "No garment," replied Majnun, "is worthy of my beloved and no garment is better for me than a sheep-skin. I desire a skin from a sheep and thus burn wild rue to scare away the evil eye. Satin and brocade for Majnun is skin. He who holds Layla dear wears skin. I have seen the face of my beloved under the skin; how can I put on any garment other than skin?"

THE VALLEY OF KNOWLEDGE

Another steep valley now appears. It is the Valley of Mystic Knowledge,[21] which has neither a beginning nor an end. To cross this valley you will have to undergo a very, very long and tedious journey. Truly, there is no road like unto that road. However, the temporal traveller is one, the spiritual another. The soul and the body are perpetually in a state of progress or deterioration according to their strength or weakness. The spiritual path is, of necessity, therefore revealed to different people in accordance with their respective faculties. How, for instance, on this path, which was trodden by Abraham, the friend of God, could the feeble spider be the companion of an elephant? The progress of each individual will depend on the degree of perfection that each will have attained, and the approximation of each to the goal will be in accordance with the state of his heart and the strength of his will. Were a gnat to fly with all its might, could it ever equal the impetuosity of the wind? There being thus divers ways of crossing the gulf, no two birds can fly alike. On this path of spiritual knowledge each one finds a different turning. One is taken to an idol, another to the *Mihrab* (a niche in the wall of a mosque, marking the direction of Mecca). One adopts idolatry (Hinduism), whereas the other embraces the faith (Islam). When the sun of knowledge dawns on the horizon of this road, each one receives illumination according to his merit and finds the task assigned to him in the knowledge of the truth. Underneath the ocean of knowledge there are thousands of pearls of wisdom and mystery, but an expert diver is required who will plunge into the water and bring up those pearls.

When those pearls are secured, and the mystery of the essence of existence clearly revealed, the furnace of this earth will be transformed into a flower garden. The adept sees the almond through the envelope of its shell. He no longer beholds himself; he perceives only his Friend. In all that he sees, be beholds His face.[22] In every atom he perceives the whole. Under the veil his eyes contemplate mysteries which are a thousandfold as luminous as the sun. But alas! for every one who acquires the knowledge of these mysteries, thousands are lost in the search! One must be perfect indeed if his ambition is to accomplish this perilous journey and to dive deep into the stormy waters. When one feels a real longing to probe these mysteries, every moment will renew his thirst for knowledge. He will be verily consumed with the desire to penetrate these secrets, and will offer himself for sacrifice a thousand times over to attain the object.

Even when you reach the glorious throne, never cease for a moment to pronounce these words of the Quran: "Is there any more?" Plunge headlong into the Ocean of Knowledge, or at least sprinkle the dust of the road upon your head.

As for you, who are asleep (and I cannot congratulate you on it), why do you not go in mourning? If you cannot have the bliss of being united with the object of your affection, rise and at least put on mourning for separation from Him.

Ye who have not yet beheld the beauty of your Beloved, do not remain seated any longer; rise and go in search of this mystery. You should be ashamed of yourself if you do not know how to set out. How long will you remain like a donkey without a bridle?

The Man of Stone

On a mountain in China there stands a man of stone, from whose eyes streams of tears flow day and night without respite. If only a drop of those tears were to become vapour and mix with the clouds, till Doomsday you would have no rain on this earth except the rain of sorrow. This man of stone is, in reality, knowledge or divine wisdom. If you have to go as far as China to find it, go there and look for it.

In the hands of indifferent persons knowledge has become as hard to handle as stone. How long will it be misunderstood? This inn of toil (this earth) is altogether enveloped in darkness, but knowledge shines in it like a lantern to show the road. Indeed, the guide of your soul in this darkness is this soul-kindling gem of knowledge. In these dark regions which have neither a beginning nor an end you have remained, like Alexander, without a guide. Even if you have collected these precious stones in large numbers, you will regret that you did not collect more. If, on the other hand, you do not avail yourself of the opportunity to gather these precious gems, you shall be still more penitent. Whether you possess this gem or do not possess it, I shall find you always a prey to grief.

The visible and the invisible world are lost in the soul. The soul is hidden from and lost in the body and the body from the soul. When you come out of this maze, you will find the proper place for a man. If you will reach this particular place, you will acquire in a single moment the knowledge of hundreds of mysteries, but woe to you, if you lag behind in this road! You will lose yourself totally in the path of grief. Do not sleep in the night and do not eat anything during the day. Then, perhaps, the desire for this quest will be kindled in you. Seek until you lose yourself in the search and you lose even the idea of the search!

The Beloved Who Found Her Lover in the Arms of Morpheus

A lover oppressed by the anguish of love was sleeping on the earth. His beloved happened to pass by and saw him unconscious. She wrote a letter to him in such terms as he deserved and tied it to the sleeve of his garment. When the lover awoke and read the letter, his heart shed tears of blood. This was the message: "O man of sloth, arise. If you are a merchant, seek silver and gold. If you are a devotee, then be alive and awake and offer prayers throughout the night till the dawn and behave like a faithful servant. If perchance you are a lover, then be ashamed of yourself. What business has sleep with the eyes of a lover? A true lover measures the wind during the day and counts the stars and measures the moon during the night. Since you are neither this nor that, O undeserving man, do not boast of your love for me. If a lover sleeps anywhere except in his coffin, I regard him as a lover only of himself. When you have entered the path of love out of ignorance, sleep becomes you, O worthless man."

A Love-Sick Sentinel

A watchman was afflicted with love. Day and night he was restless and sleepless. A friend advised him to sleep awhile. "The function of love has been added to the office of the watchman," he answered. "How can a man sleep who is charged with these two missions? How can sleep become a watchman, especially one who is a lover? How can I sleep even for a moment? Sleep is not a thing that can be borrowed from another. Every night love sits sentinel on the sentinel and tests his fidelity. For a watchman there is no sleep. For a lover's face there is no water but the water of his eyes. Sleeplessness is the badge of a sentry. Dishonour is the mark of a lover. When from the place of sleep (the eyes) water flows ceaselessly, how can sleep find its way there?"

Slumber not, O man, if you are a seeker of truth and a man of deeds. Sleep is good for you, only if you are a man of words. Keep watch in the lane of thy heart, because there are countless thieves in this neighbourhood. Guard the evil of thy heart from these brigands. When you acquire the art of guarding this precious gem, you will soon be blest with divine love and wisdom. In this ocean of blood divine knowledge will undoubtedly be attained by man through watchfulness. He who suffers the most from sleeplessness carries a wakeful heart when he reaches the Divine Presence.

Sultan Mahmud and the Fanatic

One day Sultan Mahmud found himself in a desert where he saw a religious fanatic who had lost his heart. His head was bowed with grief and his back bent under the weight of the awful burden of his sorrow.

41

"Away with thee," said the man, when he saw the king, "or I will give thee a hundred blows. Away, I tell thee! Thou art not a king, but a man of wicked feelings. Thou art faithless towards the Creator."

"Call me not unfaithful," begged Mahmud, "speak to me in becoming manner, not otherwise."

"Did'st thou but know, thou ignorant creature," replied the fanatic, "whence thou hast fallen into this bog of the senses through thy estrangement from God, the ashes and the earth would not suffice for thee and thou wouldst throw fire unceasingly and unsparingly on thy head."

THE VALLEY OF DETACHMENT

Next comes the valley where there is neither the ambition to possess anything, nor the spiritual desire to fathom divine mysteries. Complete detachment from the world, which in this place is not worth a straw, is the essence of this stage of the journey. In this state of competency of the soul there arises a cold wind so violent and fierce that it devastates a continent in one moment. The seven oceans are reduced to a mere pool of water; the seven planets appear to be but a mere spark; the seven heavens but a corpse; the seven hills but frozen snow. Then behold the wonder which reason cannot comprehend! The ant gains the strength of a hundred elephants, while a hundred caravans perish in the twinkling of an eye. In order that Adam might receive the celestial light, millions of angels clad in green were consumed with sorrow. In order that the most holy Noah might become a carpenter (of God, for making the arc), thousands of creatures were deprived of their life. Thousands of gnats fell upon the army of Nimrod in order that Abraham might be triumphant. Thousands of children were destroyed in order that Moses might see the Lord. Thousands of people were put under the yoke of Christianity, so that Christ might become the confidential possessor of the secrets of God. Millions of souls and hearts were pillaged so that Muhammad might ascend one night to heaven. In this valley neither new nor old has any value. You are free to act or not to act.

Although you see here a whole world on fire, ablaze to its very core, I know that it is no more than a dream. Should myriads of souls be drowned ceaselessly in the boundless deep, it would be like a tiny dew-drop falling into the sea. Were millions of individuals to fall victims to eternal sleep, it would be like an atom disappearing with the shadow in the sun. Should heaven and earth be split up into minute atoms, take it that a leaf has fallen from a tree. If everything from the fish to the moon were plunged into annihilation, take it that the leg of an ant has been maimed in the bottom of a well. Even though all of a sudden the two worlds were to be obliterated, it would be like the loss of a single grain of sand. If there remained no trace of men or spirits, put up with it as though it were no more than the loss of a rain-drop. Were all forms to vanish from the earth, were not even a single hair of a living being to survive, what is there to fear? In short, if the part as well as the whole were totally obliterated, it would be equivalent to a mere straw disappearing from the face of the earth. Even though the nine Cupolas of the universe were to fall down and disappear in one and the same place, it would be like a drop of water falling in the seven seas.

An Analogy from Astrology

You must have seen a learned astrologer placing before him a tablet covered with sand. He draws on it figures and pictures and shows on it the position of the stars and the planets, the heaven as well as the earth. Sometimes he presages from the position of the heavenly bodies and sometimes from the position of the earth. He traces also on this tablet the constellations and the signs of the Zodiac, the rising and the setting of the stars, deduces from them good and bad omens and draws the house of birth or of death. When in consonance with these signs he has prepared the horoscope showing good or ill luck, he sets aside the tablet and scatters the sand. No trace remains of all those drawings and pictures.

The surface of the earth is similar to this tablet. If you do not possess the strength to resist the temptations of this world, go, turn away from it and sit in a corner. If you have not got the necessary vigour to endure the hardships of this road, were you all stone, you would not weigh one straw.

The Fly and the Bee-Hive

A fly was in search of food. She saw a bee-hive in the corner. Intoxicated with the desire for the honey, she cried, "Is there a generous man who would take from me a grain of barley and place me in the midst of the bee-hive? When the tree of union will thus bear fruit, will there be anything sweeter than honey?" A passer-by took pity on her and placed her in the midst of the honey without taking the price for it. When the fly found itself in the midst of the bee-hive, her feet stuck tight in the honey. The more she fretted and struggled to set herself free, the firmer became her fetters. She cried in distress, "Alas! I am killed by violence. For me this honey has proved more bitter than poison. I offered one grain of barley to get it. I now offer ten grains for deliverance from this misery."

"None should remain inactive in this valley for a moment," continued the Hoopoe. "Let none enter it who has not come of age. It is a long time since you have been living a life of ease and ignorance, oh my friend! Your life has been brought to an end without serving any useful purpose; where is another life in which to acquire knowledge? Arise then, cut through this arduous valley and then cut yourself free from your soul and your heart. As long as you do not renounce the one or the other, you will be distracted more and more every moment. Sacrifice your soul and your heart in this road. If not they will turn you away from the path of Independence."

Too hard a mystery was this to comprehend. The Hoopoe, therefore, concluded his discourse with this anecdote:

A disciple requested his master to favour him with a word of wisdom. "Leave me in peace," said the teacher. "I will tell you nothing, until you wash your face. Of what use the scent of the musk in the midst of filth? Of what avail words of wisdom to the drunken?"

THE VALLEY OF UNITY

After the Valley of Detachment comes the Valley of Unity, the region in which everything is renounced and everything unified,[23] where there is no distinction in number and quality. All who raise their heads in this wilderness draw it from the same collar. Whether you see many individuals in it or a small number, in reality they are but one; as all this group of individuals merely compose only one, this group is complete in its oneness. That which appears to be a unit is not different from that which appears to be a quantity. As the Being of whom I speak is beyond unity and reckoning, withdraw your eyes from death and eternity. There is no place here for death, none for eternity. These two extremities having vanished, cease to speak of them. In fact, as all that is visible is nothing and nothing everything, how can all that we behold be anything but worthless in its origin and unworthy of our attention?

A man asked a Sufi one day to give him some indication of what this world is. "This world full of honour and infamy," said he, "resembles a honey-comb on which are imprinted a hundred colours. If anyone squeezes it in his hands it will become a mere mass of wax. As it is all wax and nothing else, go and rest satisfied that all these colours are also nothing."

When everything is "one," cease talking of "two." Here there is no "I," nor "Thou."[24]

Advice Given to a Shaykh by a Woman

An old woman went one day to Abu Ali and offered him a leaf of gold paper.

"Accept this, O Shaykh," she said, "at my hands."

"I have taken a vow not to accept anything from anyone save Allah," replied the holy man.

"Where hast thou learnt to see double?" at once retorted the woman. "Thou art not a man on this path with power to unite or disunite. If you see many objects, are you not squint-eyed? The eye of man does not regard anything as alien in this path. There is neither Ka'bah here nor Pagoda. One ought never to see any other than the Infinite Being and ought not to recognize any one except Him as permanent. One is in Him, by Him, and with Him, and, how strange, one is also away from these three points of contact! Whoever is not lost in the ocean of unity, were he Adam himself, is not a man. Whether one belongs to the good or the wicked, one always possesses the sun of grace within the pale of the invisible world, At last a day will dawn when that sun will take you with him and throw aside the veil which covers it. Know, then, for certain that whoever has found this sun sees neither good nor evil. So long as thou existeth individually, good and evil will exist for thee, but when thou hast merged thyself in the sunlight of the divine essence, all will be love. If thou laggest behind in thy individual existence, thou wilt see a good deal of good and a good deal of evil on the weary road of thy existence. Thou wilt be a slave to individuality so long as thy eyes rest on nothingness, so long as thou hast not been blest with the vision beatific. Would to God thou wert now what thou wast before, devoid of existence as an individual. Wash thyself clean of evil qualities; then go to the earth with the wind in thy hand. Little doth thou know what filth and impurity there is in your body. The serpent and the scorpion are within thee, behind the veil; they are asleep and apparently dead, but touch them ever so lightly and each one of them will exhibit the strength of a hundred dragons. For each of us there is a hell full of serpents. If thou art inactive, they are horribly active. If thou art armed against these unclean beasts and come out victorious in thy struggle with them, thou wilt sleep peacefully on the earth; otherwise these snakes and scorpions will bite thee violently, even under the dust of the grave, until the day of Judgment."[25]

Let us turn once more to the mysterious Valley of Unity. When the spiritual pilgrim enters this valley, he will be lost, because the Real Being will become manifest. He will remain silent because the Real Being will speak. His self being obliterated, he will be unable to understand who he is and where he is. What was but a part becomes the whole, or rather it becomes neither part nor whole. It becomes a figure without body or soul. Out of every four things, four things will come forth; and out of every hundred thousand, a hundred thousand. In the school of this wonderful secret you will see thousands of intellects with lips parched for lack of speech. What is reason here? It stands still on the threshold of the gate like an infant born blind and deaf-mute. He who has learnt a little of this secret turns away from the two worlds, but although he does not exist as an individual being, he still exists. Existence or no existence, this man still survives.[26] Give up, then, the thought of separation. Lose the thought of being lost. Then wilt thou attain unity.

THE VALLEY OF BEWILDERMENT AND STUPEFACTION

Next comes the Valley of Stupefaction. Here one is a prey to perpetual sadness. Every sigh is like a sword here, and every breath a piteous plaint. Here, alas! one sees blood dropping from the end of every hair, even though it has not been cut. There is lamentation, sorrow and consuming desire. It is at the same time day and night, but it is neither day nor night. There is fire in this place, and one is overcome, burnt and consumed thereby. How, in this bewilderment, will a man be able to set foot in this path? He will be as it were dead with astonishment and will get lost on the road. But he who has the impression of unity engraved in his heart forgets all and forgets himself. Ask him, "Art thou, or art thou not? Hast thou or hast thou not the consciousness of existence? Art thou in the midst, or art thou not? Art thou on the border? Art thou visible or invisible, perishable or immortal? Art thou the one or the other, or neither the one nor the other? Lastly, art thou thou or art thou not thou?" To these questions the poor bewildered soul will reply: "I know absolutely nothing of these things. I know neither this nor that. Nay, I know not myself. I am in love, but I know not with whom. I am neither a Musalman nor an infidel. What am I then? I am not even conscious of my love. My heart is at once both full and void of love."

A Mother's Grief

⊕ A mother was weeping over her daughter's grave. On seeing her a passer-by exclaimed: "This woman is more fortunate than men are, for she knows what we do not know. She knows from whom it is that she is cut off, and of whom she is deprived and rendered desolate. Happy is he who understands his condition and knows for whom his tears are shed! As for me, grief-stricken and afflicted, how painful is my condition! Day and night I sit and mourn. I know not for whom it is that my tears come forth like rain. So great is my grief that I do not even know whom I have lost, and for whom this terrible suffering. This woman has the advantage over thousands such as I am, because she has found the secret of the being she has lost. It is a pity that I have not found the secret, and my blood is shed with my grief and I perish in bewilderment. In such a place where there is no trace of the heart—nay the place itself has become invisible—reason has let go the reins and I can no longer find the gate to the dwelling-place of thought. Whoever arrives in this place will lose his head in it. He will find no gate to this four-walled enclosure. Should, however, anyone succeed in finding the path, he would immediately discover the whole of the secret he seeks."

The Lost Key

A Sufi once heard a man saying, "I have lost a key. Has any one found it anywhere? The door of my house is shut and I am without shelter in the street. If the door remains closed, what shall I do? I shall be for ever miserable. What shall I do?"

"Who wishes you to be miserable?" asked the Sufi. "Since you know where the door is, go and stay near it, even though it be closed. If you sit near it for a long time, there is no doubt that some one will open it for you. Your condition is not so bad as mine. My soul is consumed in stupefaction. Of the enigma that bewilders me there is no solution. There is neither a door nor a key for me."

Would to God the Sufi could set out in all haste and find the door either open or closed! None can know, none can even imagine, the real state of things. To the man who asks, "What shall I do?" reply "Do not do what you have done. Do not behave as you have behaved up to this moment."

Whoever enters the Valley of Bewilderment finds himself at every moment in a state of grief. How long shall I endure this affliction? Others have lost the way in this wilderness, how shall I get a clue to the road? I do not know it, but would to God I knew it. Aye, if I knew it, I should be in a state of stupefaction. Here, the cause for a man's complaint is the source of thanksgiving. Infidelity has become faith and faith infidelity.

THE VALLEY OF
POVERTY AND ANNIHILATION

Last comes the Valley of Poverty and Annihilation. How can one describe this steepest of steep valleys? The essential features of this valley are forgetfulness, dumbness, deafness and distraction. Here, under a single ray of the spiritual sun, you see countless shadows that surrounded you vanish. When the ocean of immensity begins to ruffle its waves, how can the shapes traced upon its surface endure? Both the worlds are no more than the forms which you see on the surface of the ocean. Whoever disputes this statement is labouring under a hallucination. He whose heart is lost in this ocean is lost for ever, and reposes there in peace. In these quiet waters he finds nothing but oblivion. If it be ever permitted to him to return from this oblivion, he will understand what is creation, and many a secret will then be divulged to him. As soon as experienced travellers in the spiritual path and tried men of action entered the realm of love, they went astray at the very first step. Of what use then was talking of this road since none of them was able to take the second step? They were all annihilated at the first step, whether they belonged to the mineral kingdom or were worthy descendants of Adam. Aloes and firewood are both equally reduced to cinders when put on the fire. In appearance they look like one and the same substance, and yet their qualities are quite different. Were an unclean object to fall into an ocean of rosewater, it would still remain impure by reason of its innate qualities. On the other hand, if something pure were to fall into this ocean, it would lose its individual existence and be identified with the motion of the ocean's waves. Ceasing to exist separately, it would thenceforward remain beautiful. It exists not and yet exists. What is this mystery? It is beyond reason to comprehend.

In this stage of the pilgrim's journey, the movement of the traveller and the motion of the ocean are the same. He is and he is not. How can that be? Who can explain this mystery? The mind cannot conceive it. In order that you may understand it, it is essential that not one hair of self shall remain with you, otherwise the seven hells will be filled with this one hair (one thought of self-consciousness).

Nasir-Ud-Din Tusi's Advice to His Disciple

One night the famous saint of Tus, that ocean of spiritual secrets, said to his disciple: "Melt perpetually. If in the path of love you waste away continually, your body will through weakness become as thin as a hair and then you can easily find a place in the ringlets of your beloved. Whoever becomes a hair in search of his beloved, doubtless becomes one of the hairs of the beloved. If you are gifted with spiritual insight, penetrate this mystery of hair in hair. If of your self even a tip of a hair remains, seven hells will be filled with that sin of yours."

He who renounces the world to tread this path finds death. When he loses all consciousness of death, he attains immortality.[27] O my heart, if you feel bewildered, cross the narrow bridge over the burning fire. Do not give yourself up to grief, because the oil in the lamp, while burning, produces a smoke as black as an old raven. When the oil has been consumed by fire, it transcends the grossness of its existence. If you seek to arrive at this place and to attain this lofty position, strip yourself of your self first and take a passport to the world of nothingness. Throw the sheet of nothingness over your head and cover your body with the robe of nonexistence. Put your feet in the stirrup of renunciation and give reins to the horse of aimlessness towards the place where there is nothing. If you possess even the end of a hair of this world, you cannot hope to have any news of the other world. Clothe yourself in the garment of nothingness and drink the cup of annihilation. In this topsy-turvy world, put round your waist the girdle of nothingness.

He who tears himself away from himself attains fidelity. He who is annihilated in annihilation forgets that he is annihilated, is not conscious even of annihilation, enters Eternity and lives everlastingly.[28] "When I saw the rays of that sun, I was swept out of existence. Water flew back to water."[29]

The Assemblage of Butterflies in Search of the Candle

One evening the butterflies of the world gathered together, each one impelled by the desire to set out in quest of the candle. They knew nothing of the object of their desire, so they all thought it would be a good thing if any one of them could try and bring them news of the candle. One of them, therefore, proceeded to a distant castle and beheld within it the light of a candle. It then returned and opened out before the others the album of its impressions and attempted to give a description of the candle according to the measure of its intelligence. Their sage leader, however, said that the explorer had come back without an adequate idea of the nature of the candle. Another butterfly thereupon started on the mission. Approaching the candle, it touched the flame with its wings for a moment. The candle was victorious, and the butterfly was completely vanquished and singed. Returning to its friends, it tried to explain the mystery to them. The wise butterfly again interposed and said: "Your explanation is not more accurate than that given by the previous explorer." Another butterfly thereupon sprang forward, intoxicated with love, and flung itself with violence into the flame of the candle. Putting its hands (front feet) round the neck of the flame, it lost itself completely in the flame. When the fire spread over its whole body, all its limbs turned red like the flame. When the wise butterfly witnessed this sight from a distance, it said: "What can any one know of this mystery? He alone knows it and that is all." This one, who lost all trace of itself, knows more than others of this mystery of annihilation. So long as thou dost not forget thy body and soul, how wilt thou know anything of the object of thy love? He who is able to give thee the slightest indication of that object inscribes the letters of his description with the blood of his soul.

PART FOUR

Reception at the Royal Court

RECEPTION AT THE ROYAL COURT

When the birds heard this account of the difficulties in their way, they realised that the burden of their mission was too heavy for their tiny shoulders, a mere handful of bones as they were. Their souls became restless and many gave up their lives in the very first stage. The rest advanced with patience and courage, and continued their march for years. Several died on the way; others were drowned in the sea; others, again, sacrificed their souls on the summit of the mountains; several were roasted by the heat of the sun, several fell victims to the jackals and tigers in the wilderness. A good many died of thirst in the forest; others went mad with hunger and committed suicide. Some lagged behind, disabled by fatigue or wounds; others could not move forward, dazed by the wonders and mysteries of the path. Some were enchanted by the charming scenery, and began to enjoy themselves, forgetting that they were out in quest of the Simurg. Thus, of the millions who had set out upon the quest, only thirty birds succeeded in completing the journey and reaching the palace of the Simurg. Weary and worn, they were without feathers, without hair, full of pain and agony. Heart-broken, soul-stricken, they reached the seat of the sovereign. They beheld His Majesty without form or quality and beyond the reach of human intellect or understanding. Then flashed the lightning of independence and a hundred worlds were consumed in one instant. Dazed and perplexed they saw that in that realm thousands of luminous suns and millions of moons and stars were like a tiny atom of dust. "O, how strange"' they exclaimed, "when even the sun is like an obscure atom before His Majesty, how can we hope to be seen in this place! O, the pity of it! What agonies have we endured during the journey! Here, a hundred skies are like a particle of dust. It makes no difference whether we are here or not."

At last the Honourable Usher of the Royal Court came out of the palace. He saw the birds standing before him without a feather or a hair, utterly travel-stained, crippled and stupefied.

"Who are ye?" he asked. "Where do you come from, and what brings you here? What is the name of your tribe and of what use are you, a handful of bones, to the world?"

"We have come here," said the tiny beings, "because we are anxious to be admitted to the presence of the Simurg and to do Him homage as our king. It is a long, long time since we started on this journey, and only thirty of us have survived out of millions. We have come all the way full of hope that we shall be admitted to the Royal Presence."

The Chamberlain replied: "Whether you exist or do not exist is immaterial to the Sovereign of Eternity. Millions of worlds filled with myriads of creatures are like an ant at the door of the King. What then, will your place be before Him? Better return, O handful of paupers!"

The unfortunate pilgrims were so disappointed at this reply that they nearly died. They began to weep and lament and said, "If we have not permission to reach the Court of the Simurg, we have no desire to retrace our steps. Will the great King reject us with contempt upon this road? Can such an insult proceed from Him, and if it does, will it not turn into honour?"

So fervent was their grief, so heart-broken their lamentation that they were admitted to the presence of the Sovereign. But, first of all, a register was placed before them, in which every detail of the deeds that each one of them had done, or had omitted to do, from the beginning to the end, was carefully entered. Seeing this list of transgressions, they were annihilated and sank down in confusion, and their bodies were reduced to dust. After they had been thus completely purged and purified from all earthly elements, their souls were resuscitated by the light of His Majesty. They stood up again, dazed and distracted. In this new life the recollection of their transgressions was completely effaced from their mind. This was *baqā* after *fanā*, immortality after perishability, life after life's loss, eternal existence after extinction.

Now the Sun celestial began to shine forth in front of them, and lo! how great was their surprise! In the reflection of their faces these thirty birds of the earth beheld the face of the Celestial Simurg. When they cast furtive glances towards the Simurg, they perceived that the Simurg was no other than those self-same thirty birds. In utter bewilderment they lost their wits and wondered whether they were their own selves or whether they had been transformed into the Simurg. Then, to themselves they turned their eyes, and wonder of wonders, those self-same birds seemed to be one Simurg! Again, when they gazed at both in a single glance, they were convinced that they and the Simurg formed in reality only one Being. This single Being was the Simurg and the Simurg this Being. That one was this and this one was that. Look where they would, in whatever direction, it was only the Simurg they saw. No one has heard of such a story in the world. Drowned in perplexity, they began to think of this mystery without the faculty of thinking, but finding no solution to the riddle, they besought the Simurg, though no words passed their lips, to explain this mystery and to solve this enigma of *I* and *Thou*.

The Simurg thereupon deigned to vouchsafe this reply to them: "The Sun of my Majesty is a mirror. Whoever beholds himself in this mirror, sees there his soul and his body, sees himself entire in it. Soul and body see soul and body. Since you, thirty birds, have come here, you find thirty birds in the mirror. Had you been forty or fifty, you would have beheld forty or fifty. Completely transformed though you be after your journey, you see yourselves here as you were before. At the beginning of your journey, you were numerous, but only thirty of you are able to see Me, and what you see is your own selves. How can any frail human being approach my presence? How can an ant's eye be lifted to the Pleiades? Has any one ever seen an insect lifting up an anvil or a gnat seizing an elephant with its teeth? All that you have known and seen is neither that which you have known nor that which you have seen. What you have said or heard is neither this nor that. If you have succeeded in crossing the valley of the spiritual road, if you have been able to do good deeds, you have only acted under compulsion from Me and you have thus been able to see the face of My essence and of My perfections. It is well that you have been able to do this, ye thirty birds. Remain bewildered, impatient and astonished. As for Me, I am more than thirty birds. I am the very essence of the Simurg. Annihilate yourselves in Me joyfully and gloriously so that you find yourselves in Me."

Thereupon the birds lost themselves for ever in the Simurg. The shade thus vanished in the Sun. Neither the traveller remained, nor the guide, nor the path. Finding the Simurg they found themselves and the riddle of *I* and *Thou* was solved.

The End

A BRIEF MEMOIR OF THE POET
FARID-UD-DIN ATTAR

A few words may be added concerning the author of the Persian text, Muhammad ibn Farid-Ud-Din Attar, one of the most distinguished poets and philosophers, Sufis and spiritualists, who adorn the pages of Persian literature. He was born in A.H. 513 (A.D. 1119-20) at Kakan, a village near Nishapur, and is said to have lived to the extraordinary age of 114 years.

His father was a respectable druggist (Attar) and in his youth Farid-Ud-Din followed the same profession. According to Dawlatshah, the famous biographer, Farid-Ud-Din was sitting one day at his door with a friend when a *dervish,* or religious mendicant, approached the shop. Looking closely into the well-furnished shop and inhaling the sweet scent of the odoriferous drugs and perfumes with which it was loaded, the mendicant heaved a deep sigh and began to shed tears. He was obviously moved by the thought of the transitory state of all earthly prosperity and the instability of human life. Attar, however, mistook the cause of the man's agitation and thought he was simply trying to excite pity to get alms. He therefore asked the dervish to move on. "Yes," said he, "there is nothing to prevent me from leaving your door or indeed from bidding adieu to this world at once. My sole possession in this world is this worn-out garment and I can give it up at any moment, but oh! Attar, I grieve for thee. How, indeed, canst thou ever bring thyself to think of death, casting all these worldly goods behind thee?"

To this story of Dawlatshah the author of *Haft Iqlim* adds an extra-ordinary denouement. According to this authority, Attar told the *dervish*

that he hoped and prayed that he also would die in poverty and content-
ment as a *dervish*. "We shall see," said the mendicant, and he placed the
wooden bowl that he held in his hand on the ground, laid his head upon
it, chanted the name of God and forthwith gave up his life to his Creator.

According to both accounts the result was the same. Attar was deeply
moved by the words of the mendicant, gave up his business, renounced all
worldly concerns, became a disciple of the famous Shaykh Rukn-Ud-Din
and applied himself assiduously to the study of Sufi philosophy. Within a
short time he showed such proficiency in the knowledge of mysticism and
such keenness in the observance of its doctrines that he came to be regard-
ed as "the scourge of all idle adepts in Sufism," whilst "his burning zeal in
the service of God became a bright lamp for the guidance of the divers for
the pearls of truth in the sea of mystic knowledge." He then travelled
extensively in the East, visiting Damascus, Egypt, India, and Turkestan,
made a pilgrimage to the holy places in Arabia, and acquired the reputa-
tion of possessing more knowledge of the Sufi philosophy and of its pro-
fessors than any contemporary author. Renowned as he was as a poet, he
acquired still greater fame by his philosophical and Sufistic writings.

Attar was the most voluminous writer of his age. In the sphere of
Sufi poetry he was the successor of the first mystic poet Sanai and the pre-
decessor of the most distinguished of Sufi poets, Jalal-Ud-Din Rumi. He
composed about 120,000 couplets of poetry, in addition to several prose
works. Of these the best known are the *Mantiq-ut-Tayr* (The Conference
of the Birds), *Pand Namah* (The Book of Counsel), *Ilahi Namah* (The Book
of God), *Asrar Namah* (The Book of Secrets), *Diwan-i-Attar* (A collection
of Odes), *Tazkirat-ul-Awliya* (The Memoirs of the Saints) and *Lisan-ul-
Ghaib* (The Hidden Voice).

A Sufi being asked to whom he ascribed greater proficiency in mystic learning, Jalal-Ud-Din Rumi or Farid-Ud-Din Attar, replied: "The

former, like an eagle, flew up to the height of perfection in the twinkling of an eye; the latter reached the same summit, but it was by crawling slowly and perseveringly like an ant."

The death of this saint was as glorious as was his earthly career. When Attar was 114 years of age, Chengizkhan invaded Persia. Attar fell into the hands of one of the Moghul soldiers, who was about to put him to death, when another Moghul, out of consideration for his age and matchless piety and his resignation in the face of death, offered to purchase his life for a thousand dirhams. The bargain would have been sealed had not Attar, anxious to see the bird of his soul released from its carnal cage, exclaimed: "Do not accept this paltry sum. You may depend upon getting a better offer." After some time, another Moghul approached, and seeing that the old man would not be of much service offered a bag of fodder as his price. "This is my full value," said Attar, "now you may sell me." This enraged the soldier so much that he murdered the sage on the spot. Thus Attar had the supreme gratification of dying a martyr.

When the chief Qazi of Nishapur lost his son, his friends suggested that the resting place of the deceased should be at the foot of Attar's sepulchre so that "the propinquity of the remains of so holy a man might ensure for him a seat in paradise." The Qazi, however, spurned the suggestion to place his son's remains at the feet of a mere reciter of tales and verses. He, therefore, selected another site for the burial. On the following night he saw in a dream Attar's tomb glowing with celestial lights and encircled by the souls of the sanctified. The dead son of the Qazi then appeared on the scene and reproached his father for not allowing him to be interred in the vicinity of so sanctified a sepulchre, and besought him to transfer his coffin to the sacred spot. The Qazi woke up, distressed and penitent, and placed his son's corpse close to the feet of Attar. He also erected a handsome monument over the Shaykh's grave.

The praise of such a mystic was on every tongue. "Attar," says Jalal-Ud-Din, "was the soul itself, and I Sana'i its two eyes. I came after both Sana'i and Attar."

Finis

NOTES

1. The famous bird that in Sufi poetry signifies the Supreme Being and is an emblem of plurality in unity.

2. This refers to the verse in the Quran in which the faithful are asked to go in search of knowledge, even to China—a very laborious journey when there were no mechanical means of transport.

3. It will be understood that these birds represent human beings in different grades of life. The peculiar excuses which each of them put forward are typical of the excuses of divers types of human beings for pursuing worldly pleasures and comforts.

4. The beauty of the king stands for "divine splendour." It is one of the Sufi sayings that "if Gnosis were to take visible shape, all who looked therein would die at the sight of its beauty and loveliness and goodness and grace and that everything bright would become dark beside its splendour."

5. A peculiar Persian expression signifying the loss of a lover's reason in the labyrinth of the ringlets of his mistress. "The story of the curl of the Beloved," says the author of *Gulshan-i-Raz*, "is very long." He, however, explains the mystery in a few charming verses from which the following are selected:

> Ask not of me the story of that knotted curl,
> It is a chain leading mad lovers captive.
> Last night I spoke straightforwardly of that stately form,
> But the tip of the curl replied, "conceal it."
> Thence crookedness prevailed over straightliness
> And the enquirers' path was hoisted away.
> By that curl all hearts are enchained,
> By that curl all souls are borne to and fro.
> A hundred thousand hearts are bound on every side,
> No heart escapes from the yoke thereof.
> If He shakes aside those black curls of His,
> No single infidel is left in the world.
> If He leaves them continually in their place,
> There remains not in the world one faithful soul.

6. The poet here moralizes in this strain: "Beware, ye hearers, the Shaykh was not the only man whose folly left him grovelling in the mire. Such a danger lurks in everybody's career. These pigs which are symbolic of man's weakness and infatuation for worldly things, will confront you in every path you tread. Especially, when you start on the pilgrimage of Sufism, you will find myriads of similar idols and pigs at every stage, and if you do not wish to be reduced to the pitiable state of the Shaykh, plunge from the commencement into the wilderness of love, kill all the pigs that you have been harbouring in your self and burn the idols that you have installed therein."

7. This story of the Shaykh, says the poet, must be listened to, not with the ordinary ears of flesh and bone, but with the ear of the heart and the soul. To understand it you must have the powers of penetration of the soul, not the ordinary faculties of comprehension.

8. Repentance is the first stage of a Sufi's journey and it marks the commencement of a new life. It is the awakening of the soul from the stupor of heedlessness, making the sinner conscious of his shortcomings. According to the *Kitab-al-Luma'*, the oldest treatise on Sufism, the Path of the Sufi pilgrim consists of the following seven stages, each of which (except the first) is the result of the stage immediately preceding it: (1) Repentance. (2) Abstinence. (3) Renunciation. (4) Poverty. (5) Patience. (6) Trust in God. (7) Satisfaction.

After each of these stages has been traversed, the traveller is raised to the higher planes of consciousness called Gnosis (*ma'rifat*) and the Truth (*haqiqat*) where the seeker (*talib*) becomes the knower or gnostic (*arif*) and realizes that knowledge, knower, and known are One.

Repentance is the act of divine grace and only those favoured by *Allah* can hope to take this preliminary step toward spiritual progress. Someone said to *Rabi'ah*: "I have committed many sins. If I turn in penitence towards God, will He turn in mercy towards me?"

No," she replied, "but if He will turn towards thee, thou wilt turn towards Him."

In this stage of repentance the novice is asked to think with remorse of his sins and to atone for them. It is, however, an esoteric doctrine of the Sufis imparted to adepts that real penitence consists in forgetting everything, one's sins included, except God. "The penitent" observes Hajwari, "is a lover of God and the lover of God is in contemplation of God. In contemplation it is not right to remember sin, for the recollection of sin is a veil between God and the devotee."

9. *Nafs*, or the lower self, the seat of passion and lust. The most appropriate English equivalent for it is "the flesh." It forms the greatest obstacle in the spiritual path. "Thy worst enemy," said the prophet of Islam, "is thy *nafs*, which is between thy two sides."

10. The *nafs* of Hallaj, it is said, was seen running behind him in the shape of a dog.

Several other cases are recorded in which it assumed other material forms. Muhammad ibn Ulyan, a Sufi of great renown, relates that one day something like a young fox came forth from his throat and he learnt only by divine illumination that it was his *nafs* or evil self. He trod on it, but it grew bigger at every kick. He said to this hideous fox, "Other things are destroyed by pain and blows; how is it that thou dost increase thereby?" "Because I was created perverse," it replied. "What gives pain to others is pleasure to me and their pleasure is my pain." Sometimes the evil self appears as a snake or a mouse, sometimes as a wolf or a tiger. Compare Omar Khayyam:

> Man's lusts like house-dogs, still the house distress
> With clamour, barking for mere wantonness.
> Foxes are they and sleep the sleep of hares;
> Crafty as wolves, as tigers merciless.

The mission of the *Salik*, or spiritual disciple, is to fight this beast, to purge it of its attributes and to wean it from those things to which it is attached and to make it realise the grossness of its nature and the vileness of its actions. In the words of Tennyson he must

> Move upward, working out the beast,
> And let the ape and tiger die.

11. The following story points to the same moral. A man dreamed that he saw Malik ibn Diner and Muhammad ibn Wasi being led into Paradise and that Malik was admitted before his companion. He, however, thought that the latter had a superior claim to this honour and could not understand the justice of such divine dispensation. "Yes," came the divine answer, "but Muhammad ibn Wasi possessed two shirts, whereas Malik had only one, that is the reason why Malik is given precedence."

The Sufi ideal of poverty, however, transcends that of renunciation of worldly goods. It enjoins not only lack of material things, but also lack of all thought or desire for worldly as well as spiritual bliss. No such thought or wish should divert his attention from God. To be detached entirely from the present as well as the future life and to desire nothing except the Lord of the present life and the future life—that is real poverty.

12. We come across several variants of this story in Persian literature. The most typical is that of the monarch saint Ibn Adham. His only son was a child when he left his throne and family under romantic circumstances. When the prince grew up, he yearned to meet his father. With his queen-mother and four thousand attendants the prince set out for the pilgrimage, as his father was in Mecca at that time. When he arrived there, he was informed that his father went daily to the forest to cut wood. The prince next day took the way to the forest and saw the saint carrying a pack of wood on his back to sell it in the Bazaar. The prince's heart was touched. His father also seemed to recognize him. Next day, one of the saint's disciples brought the prince with his mother into the presence of his father. Paternal love surged in his heart. He embraced his son warmly and

seated him on his lap and asked him questions concerning his study of the Quran. The prince's answers filled his father's heart with joy. Meanwhile, the people in the district gathered together to witness this strange interview and asked one another, "Now will he leave us and his noble work for the people?" The saint suddenly exclaimed, "O Lord, protect us," and the prince lay dead in his arms. "What has befallen thee, Ibn Adham?" asked the people, stricken with grief. The saint replied, "Divine inspiration came to me and whispered in my heart 'Wouldst thou now claim a selfless love for us?' and I prayed, 'O Lord, if my love for Thee is not selfless, then part one of us from the other'. The arrow hit my son.

Cf. also the following story from the life of Fudayl ibn Iyad: One day Fudayl kissed his child that had seen only four summers.

"Father, do you love me?" asked the child.

"Yes, darling," was the reply.

"How many hearts have you?" asked the prodigy.

"One."

"Then," demanded the child, "how can you love two with one heart?"

Fudayl saw that the child's words were a divine admonition to him that in his love for the little one he had strayed from his devotion to his Master. He, therefore, began to beat his head and repented of his love for the child and thenceforth surrendered his heart solely to God.

Cf. also Jaani's verses in the *Lawa'ih:*

Perchance with wealth and sons endowed thou art,
Yet with all these ere long thou wilt have to part.
Thrice happy he who gives his heart to One,
And sets affection on the men of heart.

13. At this stage the poet thus moralises: "Beware, ye hearers of this story. You are in the same predicament as the brothers of Joseph. Were some one to strike the cup for all his life, the story of your transgressions will not come to a finish. Would to God that all your deeds of cruelty and infidelity and perfidy may be recounted to you one by one! I wonder if you would remain in your senses after you hear all the tunes of the cup. O ye, who have remained captive under this vault like a lame ant, how long will you circumvent the cup? Pass on, because it is a basin full of blood. If you remain helpless in the cup, every moment you will hear different sounds. Come out of it and pass on, ye men of discernment, otherwise you will be disgraced by the voice of the cup."

14. There is an analogous epigram in Hindustani, pointing to the same moral. The sheep cries, *"Main, Main,"* which means 'I', 'I' and in consequence falls a prey to the butcher. On the other hand, the nightingale chirps *"Mai na,"* *"Mai na,"* "Not I, not I," and therefore finds a place in everyone's heart.

Compare Hafiz:

> Sweep off the life of Hafiz as a dream,
> Whilst Thou art, none shall hear me say, "I am."

15. He only serves God who abandons self and strips himself of all selfish thought concerning the present or future life and worships God for God's sake alone. Whoever worships Him for the sake of any desire—earthly or spiritual—adores himself, not the Lord.

16. With this it is pleasing to compare the conundrum proposed by the poet Kabir: "First, I was the giver and I gave my head and soul to the Lord. Now the Lord has been the giver of His bounty in receiving me into His presence. What shall I offer to Him? Whatever I had was given away."

17. The sky that resembles a parrot in colour.

18. The same idea is reiterated by the poet in the following passage—

> No rank vainglory for me; I would sooner have pain of love, its longings,
>   its yearnings.
> Love's pain is man's sole birthright. Angels feel it although they may not feel love.
> Insipid would be the possession of both the worlds if thy heart is rid of love's
>   ecstasy of pain, its yearnings, its hopes.
> Let the infidel delight in his infidelity and the beloved in his faith.
> An atom of love's anguish would disengage Attar's heart from both.
> Then grant me, O Thou, who art my pain's relief,
> The pain of Thy love which alone is my life.

19. Love is a divine gift, not anything that can be acquired by human effort without the grace of God. "If the whole universe wished to attract love, it could not. If it made the utmost efforts to repel it, it also could not." Those who love God are those whom He loves. Junaid defined love as the substitution of the qualities of the Beloved for the qualities of the Lover. We must therefore throw off the dross of self if we wish to obtain the pure gold of love. All the love-romances of mystic poetry—the stories of Layla and Majnun, Yusuf and Zulaykha, Salaman and Absal—are allegorical expressions of the soul's passionate longing to be reunited with God.

> On my soul's lute a chord was struck by Love,
> Transmuting all my being into love;
> Ages would not discharge my bounden debt
> Of gratitude for one short hour of love."(Jami, *Lawa'ih*)

20. The world is a wine-house. The cups are going round eternally end every new-comer

has his destined cup handed to him by the divine Cup-bearer. Every cup should reveal to him a new charm in the Cup-bearer until his spirit is intoxicated with these divine love-cups and he loses his "self" in the unconsciousness that supervenes and nothing remains before his mental eye except the supreme beauty of the Cup-bearer. "Let philosophers proclaim," says Sadi, "their sense is the best gift of nature, but those who know Thee claim that the intoxication of Thy love is far sweeter."

21. The mystic knowledge which the Sufis strive to obtain is called *ma'rifat'*, as distinguished from *'ilm* denoting ordinary knowledge. It has been aptly described by Dr. Nicholson in *The Mystics of Islam* as equivalent to the "gnosis" of Hellenistic theosophy; i.e. direct knowledge of God based on revelation or apocalyptic vision. It is not the result of any mental process, but depends entirely on the will and favour of God, who bestows it as a gift from Himself upon those whom He has created with the capacity of receiving it. It is a light of divine grace that flashes into the heart and overwhelms every human faculty in its dazzling beams. A man cannot know God by the senses, for He is immaterial, nor by intellect for He is beyond the horizon of the mental eye. Reason never gets beyond the finite. Book-learning fosters conceit and philosophy sees double. Only the heart illumined by faith and divine grace receives immediate knowledge. Hence the Prophet of Islam said: "My earth and my heaven contain Me not, but the heart of my faithful servant containeth Me."

The heart, then, is the mirror in which Divinity is reflected. If we want to have clear vision of the Divine essence, we should keep this mirror untarnished by sensual impressions and passions. It is by no means an easy thing to do, but God says in the Quran, "Whosoever shall strive for Our sake, We will guide him into Our ways."

Love is the astrolabe of heavenly mysteries. It brings with it the intense conviction born of intuition. The inner light is its own evidence. It needs no external authority, no intellectual power, no articles of faith, no dogma of theology.

22. Compare the luminous verses of Jami:

> Creation's book I studied from my youth,
> And every page examined, but in sooth
> I never found therein ought save "the Truth"
> And attributes that appertain to truth.
> What mean Dimension, Body, Species,
> In Mineral, Plant, Animal degrees?
> "The Truth" is single, but His modes beget
> All these imaginary entities.

23. "Unification consists," says Jami, "in unifying the heart, that is to say, in purifying it and denuding it of all attachment to all things other than 'The Truth' most glorious,

including not only desire and will, but also knowledge and intelligence. In fact, one must quench the desire of everything wished for before and remove from the vision of intelligence all ideas and thoughts and turn the mind away from all things whatsoever, so that there remains no consciousness or thought of anything save 'The Truth' most exalted."

> Oneness, in pilgrim's phraseology,
> Is from concern with "other" to be free;
> Learn, thou, the highest "station" of the birds,
> If language of birds be known to thee.

24. The secret of Unity is that there is no other being except the Absolute Being. Compare the description given by Shabistari (*Gulshan-i-Raz*):

> But the knower is he that knows the Very Being,
> He that witnesses Absolute Being,
> He recognises no being but the Very Being,
> And being such as his own he gambles clean away.
> Your being is naught but thorns and weeds,
> Cast it all clean away from you.
> Go, sweep out the chamber of your heart,
> Make it ready to be the dwelling-place of the Beloved.
> When you depart out, He will enter in,
> In you, void of yourself, will He display his beauty.

So also Jalal-Ud-Din:

> There is no "two" unless you are a worshipper of form:
> Before Him who is without form all becomes one.
> When you regard form, you have two eyes;
> Look on His light, which is single.
> Necessarily the eye, when it falls on one,
> Itself is one; "two" is out of sight
> The light of the two eyes cannot be divided
> When a man's eye is fixed upon His light.

25. *Cf.* The injunction of the Prophet of Islam to engage in the "Great-Warfare" against the passions.

26. As the rain-drop absorbed in the ocean is not annihilated but ceases to exist individually, so the disembodied soul becomes indistinguishable from the Universal soul. "It is true," says Dr. Nicholson, "that when Sufi writers translate mystical union into terms of love and marriage, they do not, indeed they cannot, expunge the notion of personality, but such metaphorical phrases are not necessarily inconsistent with a pantheism which

excludes all difference. To be united here and now with the World-Soul is the utmost imaginable bliss for souls that love each other on earth!"

Here is Jalal-Ud-Din Rumi's description of the union:

Happy the moment when we are seated in the palace, thou and I,
With two forms and with two figures, but with one soul, thou and I.
The colours of the grove and the voice of the birds will bestow immortality
At the time when we come into the garden, thou and I.
The stars of heaven will come to gaze upon us,
We shall show them the moon itself, thou and I.
Thou and I, individuals no more, shall be mingled in ecstasy,
Joyful and secure from foolish babble, thou and I.
All the bright plumed birds of heaven will devour their hearts with envy.
In the place where we shall laugh in such fashion, thou and I.
This is the greatest wonder, that thou and I, sitting here in the same nook,
Are at this moment both in Iraq and Khorasan, thou and I."

27. Dying to self is living in God. The mystic's sole aim and desire should, therefore, be to die before he dies.

28. The last and the best stage of the Sufi's journey is to be effaced from effacement. If the thought that he is effaced from self occurs to him it is, (says Ghazali) a blemish.

29. The Sufi pilgrim first accomplishes "the journey to God," which ends in absorption (*fana*) and abiding life in God (*baqa*). He then travels down again to the phenomenal existence in the "journey from God along with God" and is conscious that he is unity in plurality (Whinfield, *Gulshan-i-Raz*).